Men of the Wild Frontier

 A TARGET BOOK

Men
of the
Wild Frontier

Edited, with commentary by Bennett Wayne

GARRARD PUBLISHING COMPANY
CHAMPAIGN, ILLINOIS

Library of Congress Cataloging in Publication Data

Wayne, Bennett.
    Men of the wild frontier.

    (A Target book)
    SUMMARY: Brief biographies of four men
instrumental in opening up new American frontiers.

    1. Boone, Daniel, 1734–1820—Juvenile literature.
2. Jackson, Andrew, Pres. U. S., 1767–1845—
Juvenile literature. 3. Crockett, David, 1786–
1836—Juvenile literature. 4. Houston, Samuel,
1793–1863—Juvenile literature. I. Title
F454.B844   973.5′092′2 [B] [920]   73–13615
ISBN 0–8116–4905–9

Picture credits:

The Bettman Archive; pp. 9, 19, 27, 43 (top), 129, 162, cover
Brooklyn Museum; p. 100
Brown Brothers; pp. 14, 32, 60, 65, 68, 80, 105, 108, 136
        (top), 143, 151
Carnegie Library, Pittsburgh; p. 39 (top and bottom right)
The Cincinnati Historical Society; p. 42 (bottom)
City Art Museum of Saint Louis; p. 113
Culver Pictures; pp. 45, 70–71, 89, 97, 154,
Davy Crockett's Almanack, 1836–1851; pp. 125, 126, 127
Hudson's Bay Company; p. 133
Kendall, Amos, Life of General A. Jackson, Harper and Brothers,
        New York, 1843; p. 43 (bottom)
Library of Congress; pp. 52, 55, 75
Missouri Historical Society; pp. 36, 39 (bottom left)
Museum of Fine Arts, Boston, The M. and M. Karolik Collection;
        p. 41 (top)
Museum of Science and Industry, Chicago; pp. 40 (bottom), 41 (bottom)
New-York Historical Society; pp. 124, 136 (bottom)
New York Public Library, Picture Collection pp. 40 (top), 42 (top)
New York Public Library, Rare Book Division; pp. 93, 122
Brass Door Galleries, Houston, Texas and American Heritage Publishing Company; p. 120
Washington University Art Collection; p. 24

Acknowledgment:

From Flatboat Days on Frontier Rivers by James McCague
(Champaign, Illinois: Garrard Publishing Company, 1968):
        Moving West

Contents

The Trailblazers

This book is about the restless ones, the men of the wild frontier. These pioneers were born and bred in the forests and on the farms of the East, but their eyes and hearts turned westward to the land between the Appalachians and the Mississippi River.

They listened to the glowing tales told by returning hunters and dreamed of the good life to be had in the nation's first West. Many of them trudged over the mountains to see the deep forests and rushing streams for themselves. They came home with a burning desire to move their families westward.

Farms were sold, and good-byes were said. Possessions were hastily packed in wagons and mule packs. Another party of settlers had started the long journey west!

Pioneers traveled on the National Road and down the Great Road to the Wilderness Trail. They sailed west on the broad Ohio River. All of them faced terrible dangers along the way—Indian raids, fierce storms, attacks by wild animals. At the end of the trail—in Kentucky or Tennessee or in Ohio country, perhaps—there was still more danger and backbreaking work. But there was adventure too and fertile land as far as a man could see. And when that was used up, why, one could always move farther west to new frontiers!

Here are the adventure-filled life stories of some of the greatest frontiersmen of the American past: Daniel Boone, woodsman and trailblazer; Andrew Jackson, who brought to the presidency the frontier's toughness and independence; Davy Crockett, mighty hunter and teller of tall tales; and Sam Houston, who found new worlds to conquer in Texas.

Their biographies are the story of the frontier itself—its hardships, its dangers, its loneliness—and of the pioneers whose courage made the frontier part of a growing nation.

DANIEL BOONE
(1734–1820)

started looking for new frontiers when
he was still a boy. Young Daniel moved
with his family from Pennsylvania to the
wild country of North Carolina where he
became a hunter of game and furs.
He married Rebecca Bryan in 1756 and
settled down to farm, but Daniel's love
of the wilderness still drew him westward. When he heard about the fertile
lands and deep forests of Kentucky, the
sturdy frontiersman just had to go and
see it for himself. His exploration
there resulted in the opening of the
Wilderness Trail through Cumberland
Gap and the founding of the tiny settlement of Boonesborough. Here Daniel
and his family settled, and here he
brought other pioneer families. He
defended the settlers against Indian
attacks, he hunted, and he explored the
land he called a paradise. In time Daniel
moved onward to new frontiers farther
west, but his adventures in Kentucky
had already made him an American
legend.

Daniel Boone
Taming the Wilds
by Katherine E. Wilkie

1. Daniel's Indian Friend

Daniel Boone was a boy who lived on the edge of the deep woods in Pennsylvania. At that time the United States still belonged to England.

Friendly Indians often came out of the woods to visit the white men. Daniel liked the Indians. He liked them so well that he wished he could live with them.

One day in 1745 he was taking care of his father's cattle. The pasture was several miles from the settlement. Today Daniel felt lonely. He lay on a hillside and sang aloud. He wanted to hear a voice, even if it was only his own.

There was a low laugh behind him. Daniel sprang to his feet. A tall, slim Indian boy stood a few feet away. The white boy liked him at once.

"I sing, too," the young Indian said.

He threw back his head and sang. Daniel could not understand a word.

"I sing to the sun and the wind and the rain," the boy explained.

"I like your Indian song," Daniel said, "but I'm glad you speak English."

The boy patted the bow that hung over his right shoulder. "You like this?"

The bow was strong and shining. Daniel ran a finger along the smooth wood.

"I like it very much," he said.

The other boy took an arrow and placed it on the bowstring. He pulled back the bow. The arrow flew away.

"You get it," the Indian said.

Daniel ran after the arrow. He picked it up and looked back. The Indian boy was right beside him. He took the arrow from Daniel. Again he shot it. Again the white boy ran after it. The young Indian ran beside him.

He shook his head when Daniel handed him the arrow. He handed Daniel the bow. "Shoot!" he said.

Daniel took the bow in his hands. He pulled it back and let the arrow fly. By now Daniel had forgotten the cattle. He had forgotten everything but the wonderful bow, his new friend, and the wide, wild woods.

After a while the boys came to a high hill. At the bottom was an Indian village. The brown-skinned boy took Daniel by the hand and ran toward the settlement.

Several dogs barked at them. Some women were hoeing their gardens. They hardly looked up as the boys passed. An old woman was stirring something in an iron pot over a fire. It smelled good. Daniel remembered that he had eaten nothing since breakfast.

His friend stopped and pointed to Daniel and himself. The old woman nodded. With a sharp stick she lifted a piece of meat from the pot. The Indian boy took a broad leaf from a nearby bush. The woman dropped the hot meat on it.

Now Daniel knew what to do. He too found a leaf. The woman gave him some meat. Soon the hungry boys had finished their lunch.

That afternoon they swam in the clear, broad river. Then they lay on the bank in the sunshine. Daniel had never been so happy. However, he knew he must soon go home. His mother would worry if he did not return before dark.

"I must go now. I must drive the cows home," he told his Indian friend.

The boy frowned. "Women's work," he told Daniel.

Daniel laughed. "It may be for the Indians, but it's not at the Boones' house. I think I'd like being an Indian. An Indian boy has more fun than a white boy."

"There is much for an Indian to learn," the other told him. "We must learn to hunt, track animals, fish, and find our way in the wilderness."

"Those things are not work. They are fun," Daniel

told him. "I wish I were an Indian. I believe I'd make a better Indian than a white boy."

When Daniel reached home at last, his mother scolded him.

"You should not have gone off with that Indian boy. You can't trust the Indians," she told her son.

"He was a nice boy. I liked him," Daniel said.

His mother shook her head. "Indians are not like us. We think differently than they."

Daniel said nothing. But he thought his mother was mistaken.

"I believe I can think like an Indian," he said to himself. "Except for color I'm more like an Indian than a white boy."

2. Moving On

Several years went by. Then in 1750 Daniel's father called the family together. "Pack your things," he told them. "We are leaving here. Boones never stay long in one place. Besides, our farm land is worn out. We can buy rich land cheap to the south-west of here. We will settle there."

Fifteen-year-old Daniel was happy. "I'm glad we are going," he said. "I feel crowded here. There are too many houses and too many people. And the game is getting scarce."

When their land became less fertile, the Boones,
like other families, moved to new frontiers.

Daniel's father made ready for the journey. He got
out the big wagon and hitched two horses to it.
Daniel's mother packed clothes, quilts, dishes, pots,
pans, and kettles. She would fix food for the family
along the way. Daniel tied a cow behind the wagon.

The family said good-bye to the neighbors and to
their old home and started off. Mother, the girls, and
the little children rode in the wagon. Father and
the boys took turns riding the horses. Sometimes all
of the Boones walked so that the horses could rest.
Father and the boys had guns to kill birds and small
animals for food along the way.

The Boones traveled across Pennsylvania. On and on they went toward the new country. Daniel caught many rabbits, which his mother stewed. Once he shot a small black bear. Another time he killed a deer. This gave the Boones food for several days.

At last the family came to the rolling, green Yadkin Valley in North Carolina. There were a few houses there already, but it was much wilder than in Pennsylvania.

Father said, "This is good farming land. We will stop here."

Daniel looked all about him. There was level land close by. There were woods not far away. And there were mountains in the west. Daniel knew the hunting would be good.

"I like this place," he said. "There's plenty of room here."

Father and the boys jumped off the horses. Mother and the girls climbed down from the wagon. They fed the horses and the cow. They made a campfire. Father and the boys cut down trees and started to build a log house. Soon the Boones had a new home in the new land.

The years went by. Daniel grew taller. His shoulders became wider. He was fair haired and blue eyed, lean and rugged. He hunted in the woods of the Yadkin Valley. He often brought home deer and bear. The Boones' neighbors said that Daniel was the best shot for miles around. Daniel Boone had grown up.

3. A Knock at the Door

When Daniel Boone was a young man, there was a war between England and France. England sent troops to fight against the French in America. The French claimed the land west of the Appalachian Mountains. The English claimed the same land. The Indians sided with the French.

Daniel Boone drove a supply wagon for a group of English and American soldiers. He made friends with another young wagoner named John Finley. Finley had been to the land southwest of the mountains. Each night he and Boone sat by the campfire and talked.

"I've been deep in the wilderness they call Kentucky," Finley told Boone. "It's a wonderful place. The forests go on and on and on. There are thousands of buffalo in Kentucky. There are deer, bear, and small animals, too. It's a great land for hunters."

"I want to go there," Daniel said.

"There are Indians in the wilderness," Finley told Daniel. "They live to the north and the south of

Kentucky. They call the land their hunting ground. They do not like white men to go there."

"There should be room enough for both Indians and white men," Daniel Boone replied. He thought for a while. "Someday I am going to Kentucky."

When Daniel went back home to the Yadkin Valley, he married a tall, dark-haired girl named Rebecca Bryan. Sometimes he liked to tease her. One summer day before they married, he was sitting beside her under a big tree. As they talked, Daniel absentmindedly cut the grass with his broad-bladed knife. Suddenly he cut a long slit in her fresh white apron.

"Why did you do that, Daniel?" she asked in surprise.

His blue eyes twinkled. "I guess I wanted to see if you had a bad temper," he said.

Even though her pretty apron was ruined, Rebecca wasn't angry. Daniel felt that she would make a good wife. Life in the wilderness was often difficult and dangerous. He wanted a wife who did not become upset easily.

They were married, and soon the first of their many children arrived. Daniel loved his children. As soon as his son James was old enough, he taught him to hunt.

In the spring and summer Daniel would farm. In

the autumn he hunted, and in the winter he trapped. He made long trips in the forest and brought home food for his family and valuable furs and deer skins. Many of these he sold. He enjoyed exploring as much as he enjoyed hunting. Once he even went as far south as Florida with the idea of settling there. But he was disappointed in the land. He longed to explore Kentucky, but he did not want to go alone.

One day the Boone family heard a knock at the door. It was Boone's old friend, John Finley.

"Let's go to Kentucky, Daniel!" he said.

"Let's!" Daniel agreed. "I think about it all the time. You know how much I love the wilderness. That's the one place I really feel at home."

4. On to Kentucky

Early in 1769, Daniel Boone, John Finley, and four other strong men started for Kentucky. One of the men was Daniel's brother-in-law. They took their guns. They carried animal traps too. They planned to bring back skins and furs to sell.

The hunters rode their horses across the mountains. Soon they came to the Cumberland Gap, a mountain valley which led into Kentucky. The Indians used the gap also, but the white men did not see any of them at this time. It was weeks before they saw a single Indian.

But they did see rich, green meadows which stretched ahead for miles. Silver rivers wound like ribbons through them. In some places there were low rolling hills and in others great towering mountains. The woods were thick and still. The sunlight made dancing patterns on the pine needles. Kentucky was as beautiful as John Finley had said.

Everywhere they went the men found lots of game. There were deer and buffalo. There were fur-bearing animals such as mink and otter and beaver. There were many different kinds of birds.

From a mountaintop near Cumberland Gap, Boone and his men had their first glimpse of Kentucky.

When the men went hunting, they separated into pairs. One winter day Boone and his brother-in-law were captured by Indians. The Indians did not harm them, but they took all their deer skins.

"Get out of Kentucky and stay out!" the Indians told them.

Daniel Boone did not scare easily. He and his brother-in-law did not want to leave Kentucky. But the other four were afraid. They returned to the settlements. Boone never saw Finley again. But Boone was soon joined by his brother, Squire, and a friend named Alexander Neeley. Squire had promised to harvest the crops back home and then join them in the late autumn with fresh horses, traps, and gunpowder. Skilled woodsmen that they were, the brothers somehow found each other in the wilderness.

While they were hunting, the men separated again. They met every two weeks. One week Boone's brother-in-law did not return to camp. He never did come back. Five years later a skeleton with a powder horn beside it was found in a hollow tree. Perhaps he was wounded by an Indian. No one really knows what happened to him.

Neeley was scared. He decided to go home alone. But Daniel and Squire stayed on all winter and spring. They hunted and trapped until they had a lot of skins. Then Squire went home to sell the skins and buy more gunpowder and traps.

Daniel stayed on in the wilderness. He did not mind being alone. He was never afraid. With his trusty rifle, Tick-Licker, over his shoulder, he explored much of Kentucky. He was happy because the wilderness was wide and he felt free. After a few months Squire came back. Again the brothers hunted together.

At last Daniel said to Squire, "I'll go home with you this time. We have all the skins we can carry."

"When we sell them, we'll have plenty of money to take to our families," Squire said happily.

It did not happen that way. Indians attacked the brothers when they were nearly home and took the skins. The Boones were still poor men. But Daniel was happy. He was glad that he had roamed the wilderness for nearly two years. He was sorry he had lost the skins, but he was happy that he had seen Kentucky.

5. Attacked by Indians

Two years later Daniel Boone decided that he had been away from Kentucky long enough.

"Pack up, Rebecca," he said to his wife. "Pack up, children. We Boones can't stay in one spot forever. We're moving to Kentucky. It's wild and beautiful there. There'll be plenty of land for you young ones when you grow up and want homes of your own."

So the Boones packed up. Six other families joined them. People always seemed ready to join Daniel in his search for adventure. The household goods and the farm tools were piled on pack horses. A few of the people rode horseback. But most of them walked. They drove their pigs and cattle before them. The rough trails made travel slow, but the families did not seem to mind.

Just before they reached Cumberland Gap, Daniel sent his sixteen-year-old son, James, on an errand.

"Turn back to Captain Russell's cabin and ask him for the farm tools he and I were talking about," Daniel told the boy. "You can catch up with us tomorrow."

James reached Captain Russell's safely. He camped that night with several men who planned to join Boone. In the darkness some Indians crept up and killed them all.

When the families with Boone heard the news, they no longer wanted to go to Kentucky. They turned and went back over the mountains. The Boone family was sad because of James's death. But Daniel would not give up his dream of living in

Kentucky. It would just have to wait a little. He took his wife and children to a spot where they would be safe. But they did not go all the way back to the Yadkin Valley.

Daniel learned that all through the Kentucky Wilderness Indians were fighting white men.

Too many white men were coming west. Indians wanted to keep their hunting ground for themselves. Daniel Boone and another man went into Kentucky to warn the surveyors who were measuring land there. Nearly all of them escaped safely. After a while, the Indians stopped fighting, and Kentucky was peaceful again.

6. The Wilderness Road

Now a rich man named Richard Henderson had an idea. He would try to buy Kentucky from the Indians for himself and start another colony. His own company would sell land to settlers. Henderson was Daniel's friend. Boone had talked to the Indians about the idea and thought they would sell the land. Many Indian tribes hunted in Kentucky, but the Cherokees were the most important. They had conquered the other tribes and ruled the land. Henderson sent Boone to ask the Cherokees to meet him at Sycamore Shoals in what is now Tennessee.

This painting by George Caleb Bingham shows Daniel Boone escorting a party of settlers to Kentucky on the Wilderness Trail.

Twelve hundred Indian men, women, and children came to the meeting place. Henderson had all his trade goods spread out. There were yards and yards of red cloth. There were hundreds of bright new guns. There were beads and pins and little mirrors for the women. Henderson's company had paid a great deal of money for the trade goods.

The Indians had no way of knowing that their land was worth much more than these trade goods. Although they had their own lawyer, they traded Kentucky to Henderson for a tiny part of what it was worth. The Cherokees warned the white men of other Indians who came hunting from the west and the north. They told Henderson he might have trouble settling the land.

Boone did not go with Henderson to Sycamore Shoals. He waited near Cumberland Gap with thirty men. When Henderson sent word that he had bought Kentucky, Boone spoke one word to his men.

"Start!" he said.

The men began to make the famous Wilderness Trail that was to lead to Kentucky. Later it would be traveled by settlers with their horses, wagons, and cattle. Just now Boone's men chose the shortest and easiest way over the mountains and through the woods. They followed Indian trails and buffalo paths. They swung their axes. They cut down trees. They crossed streams. Daniel Boone worked as hard as anyone, and all the time he kept a sharp lookout for unfriendly Indians.

The men did not stop until they reached the banks of the Kentucky River. Here they began to build a fort. Boone knew that the Shawnees and other Indian tribes would not agree that Henderson had bought Kentucky.

When Henderson came to the settlement, he said, "We will call this place Boonesborough. It is right to name it for the man who led us here."

Boone went back to get his family. Some of his children had grown up and married before the Boones set out for Kentucky the first time. Thirteen-year-old Jemima was his last unmarried daughter. She and her mother were the first white women to stand on the bank of the Kentucky river.

7. The Rescue

One Sunday afternoon Jemima and two other girls went for a canoe ride on the Kentucky River at Boonesborough. They knew they should not go out of sight of the fort, but they went anyway. They paddled down the river and around the bend. The current drew them in to the opposite bank.

Jemima Boone and her friends were captured by a band of Indians when their boat drifted to shore.

"Let's land and pick some of those bright-colored flowers," one of the girls suggested.

Jemima shook her head. "I'm afraid," she said. "The Shawnees may be close by."

By now the canoe had drifted near the shore. The girl at the bow shoved with her paddle. The boat would not move. It was stuck fast in the mud.

All at once five Indians leaped from the underbrush. They grabbed the screaming girls and carried them into the forest. They planned to take them north to the Indian towns and keep them there.

27

Back at the fort no one missed the girls until after dark. Then someone saw that the canoe was gone. When Daniel Boone heard this, he picked up his gun and rushed toward the river. He did not even stop to put on his moccasins. He felt sure that the Indians had taken Jemima and her friends away.

Boone led a rescue party to search for the girls. Three young men who loved the girls very much went along. The men took canoes and began to paddle down the river. They could not go far in the dark. Before long they had to stop and wait for morning.

When the sun came up, Boone found the girls' trail. He thought the Indians were taking them toward the Ohio River. He knew he must catch them before they crossed it and went to the Indian towns in the north.

The white men left their canoe. They traveled all day through the deep woods. Then they made camp and waited for the long night to end. At daylight they started out again.

Boone took short cuts through the woods, but he always found the trail. His sharp eyes saw what the girls had left for him to see. One had dug her heels into the soft mud. Another had left bits of her dress here and there.

Boone led the men straight through the heart of the forest to Jemima and her friends. About noon the men caught sight of the girls. The Indians had stopped with them for their noon meal. The white men crept up. Then they started shooting from the underbrush.

"It's father!" Jemima cried.

"Fall flat on your faces, girls!" Daniel Boone shouted.

The white men ran toward the Indians. They shot their rifles as they ran.

The Indians were taken by surprise. One Indian threw his tomahawk. It almost hit the girls. Two Indians were shot. The others ran away.

The rescue party took the girls back to Boonesborough. Later the girls married the three young men who had joined in the search.

8. The Fort Is Saved

Boone became known far and wide as the greatest man in the Kentucky Wilderness. One winter, about a year after he had saved the girls from the Indians, he went with some other men to a place where there were salt springs. These were called salt licks because the wild animals liked to lick the salt. The men planned to camp there several weeks. They would boil the water in big kettles until there was only salt left. Then they would take the salt back to the people at Boonesborough.

One day Boone went out hunting alone. Suddenly he was surprised by Indians. They were members of a war party led by Chief Blackfish. They were on their way to Boonesborough. These Shawnee Indians came from north of Kentucky. They felt that Henderson had no right to claim their hunting grounds. Certainly *they* had not sold Kentucky to him. They might not have been so warlike if the American Revolution had not started. The British were making friends with the Indians everywhere and helping them fight the settlers.

Boone knew how the Shawnees felt about having to share their hunting ground with the white men. But he knew also that he must find a way to save the fort.

"Don't go to Boonesborough now," he told the Indians. "You don't have a big enough war party. Boonesborough is far too strong for you to capture."

This was not true at all. There were not many men at the fort. But Daniel hoped to stall off the Shawnees until Boonesborough had time to send for help.

"Wait until spring," he went on. "Right now it is too cold for the women and the children at the fort to travel. But in the spring you can easily capture the fort and take everyone north with you."

Chief Blackfish was delighted to find that Boone was so friendly. He had admired Boone for a long time. He did not know that Boone was trying hard to fool him.

"What about your men?" Chief Blackfish asked.

Boone thought quickly. He knew the Indians had seen the men at the salt licks.

"I will lead you to my men," he told Chief Blackfish, "if you will promise not to kill them."

Chief Blackfish promised. Boone took the Indians to his men.

"We are in great danger," he whispered to them. "We must go north with the Indians, or they will kill us. The fort is in danger too. But perhaps we can escape and warn our families."

At the end of the long journey the Indians and their prisoners reached the Shawnee towns in the north. There, Chief Blackfish told Boone that he wanted him for a son. He made Boone go through a long adoption ceremony and gave him the name of Big Turtle.

Boone liked Chief Blackfish, but he did not really want to be a Shawnee. He only pretended to be pleased about becoming the chief's son.

One day the Indians went hunting. While they

were gone, Boone ran away and started for Boonesborough. The Indians followed him, but he was too clever for them. They lost his trail. In four days he traveled 160 miles. Finally he reached Boonesborough.

"The Indians are on the way! Get ready to fight!" he told the people.

Soon Chief Blackfish came with over 400 Shawnees. He called for Boone to come outside the fort. Daniel Boone went out bravely.

"Why did you run away?" Chief Blackfish asked Boone.

Boonesborough: only a log wall protected the tiny cabins.

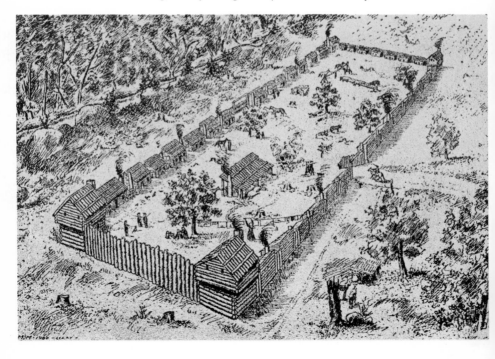

"I wanted to see my wife and my children," Boone answered.

"You have seen them," the chief replied. "Now come back with me. You and all your people."

"Give me time to think it over," Boone said.

He hoped that help would come from other forts. He waited and waited, but no help came.

"We shall defend the fort as long as a man is living," Boone told the people.

The fight began. The Indians fired at the fort. The white men fired back. Everyone worked hard. The women and the children loaded guns and carried food to the men. The white men were outnumbered, but the Indians did not know this.

The men did not stop fighting for eight days and eight nights. By then everyone was very tired. The Indians had shot flaming torches, and the roofs of the cabins were on fire. Not a drop of water was left in the fort.

"Look! Look!" someone shouted.

The sky had been dark all day. Now it was starting to rain. Before long it was pouring. The rain came down and put out the fires. It filled the tubs and buckets with water. Everyone felt hopeful again.

When morning came, no Indians were in sight. Every single one of them was gone. They had disappeared into the forest. The fort was saved.

9. Daniel Boone's Reward

The Indian raids kept on all over Kentucky. When the American Revolution ended, the British stopped helping the Indians fight the settlers. Some tribes kept on fighting on their own, but finally the settlers defeated the Indians and forced them to sign a treaty. Things slowly became more peaceful.

More and more settlers came west. They came over the Wilderness Trail that Boone and his men had made. They came down the Ohio River in big flatboats. These settlers killed game in the forest. They cleared the land, grew crops, built houses, and started towns.

Daniel Boone was 50 years old now. One day he discovered that he did not own any of the land he had thought was his.

"That's not fair," he said. "I was one of the first to come to Kentucky. My life was hard. I risked it for the people many times."

It was not fair, but it was true. Boone had been too busy hunting and trapping to put his claims on paper. Boone lost almost all his land. He tried to farm, but he was not a good farmer. He tried to keep a store, but his heart was not in it. His good wife, Rebecca, often took his place in the store, while Daniel worked as a guide showing new settlers the way down the Ohio River. He also held some jobs with the new government.

One day hunters told Daniel Boone about land farther west near the great Mississippi River. "It's wild and free," they said. "There are bear and deer. There are herds of buffalo. It's the kind of land Kentucky used to be."

"That's the place for me," Boone said. "It's too crowded here. The other day I looked out of the window and saw smoke from another man's chimney. I'll go west. I want elbow room."

Besides elbow room, he wanted land. He had always dreamed about owning a lot of land. He was disappointed about losing his claims in Kentucky.

So Boone and his family went west. The land where they settled belonged to Spain. Later it was traded to the French and then bought by the United States. It is the land we now call Missouri.

The Spaniards were proud to have Daniel Boone live among them. They gave him 10,000 acres of land. He hunted and trapped in the new country as he had in the old. He sold the furs and skins for a good price.

In 1804 the land where Daniel Boone lived became part of the United States. Boone could not prove that the land belonged to him, and again he lost his claim.

Then several years later the United States Congress voted to give Boone one thousand acres of land. It was a reward for all he had done in exploring and settling the West.

Boone sold the land which Congress had given him. He took his money and his earnings from the sale of furs and went back to Kentucky. He called together all the people he had once known.

"I owed money to you when I left here," he said. "I want to pay my debts."

When he returned to his family in Missouri, Boone was a poor man again. But he had a smile on his face.

"I am a free man," he said. "I owe nothing to any man. That makes it worth being poor again."

Daniel went on hunting and fishing until he was very old. He never stopped exploring. He was still looking for adventure and elbow room!

But Daniel Boone, traveler, hunter, woodsman, and fighter, is best remembered as the man who opened the way to Kentucky.

Daniel Boone was an old man when this portrait was painted. It showed him as the sturdy pioneer and lover of frontiers that he had always been.

To the Frontier or Bust!

At first only the most daring travelers made the trip over the Appalachians. They came in twos and threes, on foot and on horseback, over footpaths cut by the Indians and on the Wilderness Trail opened by Daniel Boone and his men. Then, as tales were carried back to the East of a promised land beyond the mountains, thousands and tens of thousands followed. They poured first into Tennessee and Kentucky and then, in the early 1800s, into the Ohio country. "All America is moving westward!" an English traveler exclaimed in wonder in 1816.

These pioneers traveled overland, by covered wagon and by stagecoach, on roads little better than the trails taken by earlier settlers. The footpaths had been widened, and sometimes roadbeds had been formed by placing small logs side by side and covering them with three or four inches of soil. For the most part, though, wagons and stagecoaches alike jostled and bumped over rough ground in dry weather and sank wheel-deep in the mud after a rainy spell.

Sometimes part of the trip was taken on the Ohio River. But passengers on the slow-moving boats floating downriver were an easy mark for hostile Indians. And their clumsy craft were often overturned and wrecked in the swift currents.

Still, on they came, these brave and hardy souls, willing to suffer terrible hardship and even to risk death to reach the frontier. There was no stopping them!

On the following pages are pictured some of the ways they traveled and the frontier they found beyond the mountains.

Crude and hastily built flatboats of every size
and variety provided traveling homes for families
and their livestock on the Ohio River.

OVERLAND BY COVERED WAGON AND STAGECOACH

Most of the settlers began the long journey west in covered wagons. At night the travelers stopped to cook food over an open fire and to sleep.

Stagecoach travel was dangerous on roads that were dotted with tree stumps. The axmen shown here widened trails and built log roads to take wheeled vehicles.

LIFE ON THE WILD FRONTIER

When pioneers reached "Kaintuck" or the Ohio country, they found land for the taking. With their axes they felled trees to build crude log cabins and forts and cleared the land for planting.

Many settlers had little interest in farming. They hunted and trapped animals in the forest for meat and furs. When Indians attacked, they used their trusty rifles to defend their homes.

ANDREW JACKSON
(1767–1845)

moved to the frontier lands of Tennessee
in 1788 to practice law. Frontier life was
rugged, but not too hard for the hotheaded young man who had fought in
the Revolutionary War when he was
only fourteen. In Tennessee the young
lawyer bought land, became a judge,
and was elected congressman from the
new state. Then his fighting spirit took
him into the militia. As an officer, he led
his men against the Creek Indians who
had attacked Fort Mims. As a major
general in the United States Army in the
War of 1812, Jackson became a hero at
the Battle of New Orleans. His toughness
as a soldier won him the nickname of
Old Hickory—and the admiration of the
whole nation. As president, Jackson
brought to the White House the fighting
spirit of the frontier. His firm belief in the
rights of the people and a strong federal
government would influence the course
of the new nation for years to come.

Andrew Jackson
Pioneer and President
by John Parlin

1. Andy Reads the News

"The Philadelphia newspaper is here!" Andy Jackson shouted as he galloped up to a farmhouse. "I'm going to read it aloud at my uncle's house this afternoon."

Andy rode his horse from farm to farm. He invited everyone in the little South Carolina settlement to hear him read the paper. Many of the grown people could not read. There had been few schools when they were children. But Andy was going to school.

Everybody wanted to hear the news. It was August 1776. America had been fighting England for many months. England ruled America. But the Americans did not like the way the English ruled.

The Continental Congress was meeting in Philadelphia. The men in Congress were the leaders of America. What they did was big news.

The news had to travel a long way. A ship brought the newspaper from Philadelphia to Charleston. Then a postman on horseback rode 160 miles to the frontier where Andy lived. It was a place called the Waxhaw settlement.

Forty farmers came to hear Andy read the newspaper. Andy stood on a chair and read in a loud,
clear voice. He told how Congress had approved the
Declaration of Independence on July fourth. The
Declaration listed the things that England's king
had done to America.

"He has . . . burnt our towns and destroyed the
lives of our people," Andy read.

"Down with the king!" one of the farmers
shouted.

Andy held up his hand for silence. "I'm almost
through," he said. "Just listen to this. 'These united
colonies are and of right ought to be FREE AND
INDEPENDENT STATES!' "

"Hooray for freedom!" a farmer yelled. "And
hooray for Andy! He's a good reader."

Andy stuck out his chest with pride. There were
some mighty big words in the Declaration of
Independence. Andy had read each one right.

The farmers knew the Declaration of Independence
meant a long war. Some of them had come to
America from England. But they loved freedom more
than they loved England.

Andy's father was Scotch-Irish. Mr. Jackson had
sailed to America before Andy was born. Andy's
mother and brothers had come with him. The
brothers were named Hugh and Bobby. Mr. Jackson

died in 1767. A few nights later, on March 15, Andrew Jackson was born. His mother took the little baby and the older boys to live on the farm with their Uncle Jim and Aunt Jane.

Uncle Jim grew vegetables and raised cattle. When Andy was big enough he helped with the cattle. He built cow pens out of hickory wood. Andy used hickory because it was so hard and tough.

One morning soon after he read the newspaper, Andy decided to go fishing. His friend, George McWhorter, went with him. As they walked to the river they looked for Indian arrowheads. Suddenly Andy spied one lying on the ground. George saw it

Uncle Jim's frontier farm in Waxhaw looked much like the newly cleared farm shown in this print.

at the same time. Andy dived for the arrowhead. But George already had it.

"I saw it first!" George shouted.

Andy doubled up his fist and hit George on the jaw. He fought like a tiger. But George was bigger than Andy. He gave Andy a bloody nose.

The boys finally stopped fighting. But Andy still would not admit that George had seen the arrowhead first. Andrew Jackson always thought he was right.

When Andy got home his mother saw his bloody nose. She knew he had been in another fight.

"What makes you so hotheaded, son?" she asked.

"Maybe it's my red hair," Andy said.

"That's a poor excuse. Next time you get angry, count to ten before you start fighting. Maybe your temper will cool off."

"Suppose I were in the American army," Andy said. "Suppose I were to see an English soldier. Should I count to ten before I shoot?"

"If you did, your aim would be better," his mother answered. "You'd have a better chance to hit him."

"But he might shoot me first," Andy said.

Andy was just daydreaming about the English soldier. The big battles were being fought in the North. However, the people in South Carolina helped by sending food to the army.

2. The War Comes Closer

When Andy was eleven, his Uncle Jim took him on a cattle drive to Charleston. Andy felt like a real man as he rode off from home. When a cow strayed from the herd, Andy galloped after it.

At night Andy sat by the campfire. The grownups often talked about fighting the Indians in the old days. A man told Andy that Indians sometimes made noises like birds to signal each other.

One night they heard an owl. It cried "Whooo, whooo!" Andy's friend made the same sound. But it wasn't exactly the same. Andy learned to tell whether the "whooo" was made by an owl or a man.

Andy was excited when they reached Charleston. He had never seen such crowded streets, such big houses, or so many buildings.

When Andy returned home, he heard that the war was coming closer. Some English soldiers had landed in Georgia. They were marching on Charleston.

A regiment of South Carolina soldiers was ordered to stop the English. Andy had an uncle who was a captain in the army. He was Uncle Bob. Andy's big brother, Hugh, was one of his soldiers. Andy and his other brother, Bobby, begged Uncle Bob to let them join the army. But he said they were too young.

The American soldiers beat the English before they reached Charleston, but Hugh did not come back. He fought hard in the battle. Soon afterwards he became sick and died.

When Andy heard the news, he cried. "Someday," he said to himself, "I'm going to make the English pay."

It wasn't long before the English came back. This time they captured Charleston.

Then some of them marched toward the Waxhaw settlement. They surprised some American soldiers near where Andy lived. They killed and wounded many Americans.

The Americans used the Waxhaw church as a hospital. The wounded men had to lie on the floor. Mrs. Jackson, Andy, and Bobby helped the wounded men. The boys brought water from a well. Then they built a fire and heated the water.

Their mother used the water to wash the soldiers' wounds. Some of the men cried with pain. This made Andy hate the English even more.

Later, he and Bobby went to see Uncle Bob again. "Please, Uncle Bob," Andy begged, "let us fight the English. We'll make good soldiers."

"How old are you, Andy?" Uncle Bob asked.

"I'm going on fourteen," Andy said, "and I'm big for my age."

This old painting shows young Andy watching in dismay as the British attack Waxhaw.

"We need every man we can get," Uncle Bob said. "I'll be glad to have you."

Andy was proud that his uncle had used the word "man." Andy had played "soldier" when he was a little boy. Now he was a real soldier in a real war.

3. Prisoner of War

Uncle Bob heard that the English planned to attack the settlement again. He told his soldiers to meet at the church.

Andy and Bobby went by horseback to the church. As they waited for orders, they saw some farmers riding toward them. They thought the farmers were friends.

But they were not friends at all. The farmers suddenly stopped by the side of the road. Behind them, many English soldiers were hiding. It was a smart trick. The English soldiers rushed toward the church. Their swords flashed in the sun.

The Americans fought bravely, but they were outnumbered. The English set the church on fire.

"Try to escape!" Uncle Bob shouted.

Andy and Bobby jumped on their horses. They raced off in different directions. An English soldier chased Andy. Andy and his horse jumped across a stream. Soon they were safe in the woods.

Suddenly, Andy heard a noise in the bushes. He held his gun ready to shoot. It might be an English soldier. Before he shot, he remembered his mother's advice.

"One," he counted, "two, three. . . ."

A horse's head poked out of the bushes. Sitting on the horse was Bobby. Andy was surely glad he had not shot!

That night, the boys camped in the woods. They had no food. The next morning they went to a cousin's house for breakfast. While they were eating, some English soldiers broke into the house. They made the boys their prisoners.

One of the soldiers ordered Andy to clean his boots.

"Clean them yourself," Andy said. "I'm a prisoner of war, not your slave!"

The English soldier lifted his sword. Andy put up his hand to protect himself. The soldier hit Andy with all his might. Blood poured from deep cuts on Andy's face and hand.

Later Bobby asked, "Wouldn't it have been better to clean his boots?"

"No!" Andy cried. "I'll never clean an Englishman's boots. They can hang me first!"

The English made the boys march 40 miles to a town called Camden. At Camden they were thrown

Fiery-tempered young Andy Jackson refuses to clean his captor's boots. A Currier and Ives print.

into prison. Many other American soldiers were there. Soon the boys caught a terrible disease. It was smallpox! Many prisoners died of smallpox.

Mrs. Jackson wanted to help her boys. She came to see an English officer at Camden. She begged him to free Andy and Bobby. She said the Americans would free some English prisoners in return. The English let Andy and Bobby out of prison.

Mrs. Jackson took her sick boys home. Bobby died soon after they got there. Mrs. Jackson nursed Andy back to health.

There was more nursing for her to do. Some

American soldiers were on English prison ships in Charleston harbor. The ships were dirty and crowded. Many soldiers were sick. Mrs. Jackson went to Charleston to nurse them. When she kissed Andy good-bye, she said, "*Never tell a lie, nor take what is not your own.*"

It was the last advice she ever gave Andy. One day, a horseman from Charleston brought Andy a small bundle. Andy opened it slowly. It held his mother's clothes and a few of her things. His mother was dead. Andy was alone in the world.

4. By Wagon to Nashville

Andy was glad when the war was over. The Americans had won. Now Andy could make his living. He decided to be a lawyer. He went to Salisbury, North Carolina, and studied in a lawyer's office.

After he learned to be a lawyer, he moved west. The Waxhaw settlement was getting crowded. A young man had a better chance to get ahead on the frontier.

Andy started for Nashville with some pioneers. They were the first group of people to take wagons over the new Cumberland Road. The road crossed 180 miles of forest. Indians roamed the woods.

At night the pioneers camped by the road. One

night some of the men sat up late singing around the campfire. Andy smiled as he listened.

Way up yonder above the moon
A blue jay nests in a silver spoon.
Way down yonder on a hollow log
A red bird danced with a green bullfrog.

Just as the song ended, Andy heard an owl cry "whooo." The cry came from north of the camp. Then Andy heard an answering "whooo" from the south. Andy jumped to his feet. He knew the sounds were made by Indians, not owls!

He felt sure the Indians planned to attack when the men went to sleep. He rushed to the campfire and cried, "Indians are all around us!"

"What will we do?" one of the singers asked.

"We'll break camp now," Jackson said. "Wake everybody up."

The Indians were afraid to attack when everyone was awake, for all the men had guns. Andy was glad that he had learned how real owls sounded.

A few days later the pioneers reached Nashville. Andy looked at the small group of cabins.

"Where's the courthouse?" he asked someone.

"Over there." The man pointed to a tiny log building. It was only eighteen-feet square.

Soon Andy was busy working at the courthouse. Though he was only 21 years old, he was a good lawyer.

Andy moved into a boardinghouse run by Mrs. John Donelson. She had a beautiful daughter named Rachel. When she was only seventeen, Rachel had married a man named Lewis Robards. They did not get along, so Rachel came back to her mother's house to live.

Rachel thought Andrew Jackson was very handsome. He was six feet tall, and very slim. She and Andrew fell in love. They were married three years later.

5. The Big Horse Race

Andrew Jackson was very busy as a lawyer. With the money he saved, he bought a lot of land. He paid only ten cents an acre for some of it. He knew that some day his land would be worth a great deal of money.

Many pioneers were moving to this part of the frontier. In those days it was called the "territory south of the Ohio River." Jackson wanted it to become a state.

He and the other leaders made plans for the new state. They decided to call it Tennessee. Finally, the United States government approved their plan. Tennessee became the sixteenth state in the Union.

Then Tennessee picked men to be in the national government. Andrew Jackson was elected to the House of Representatives in 1796.

Rachel was proud that Andrew was going to Congress. But she was sad too. She would be lonesome without him.

"If only we had some children," she sighed as she kissed Andrew good-bye.

Jackson had to ride a horse most of the way to Philadelphia. That was where Congress met then. He was one of the first men in Congress to come from the frontier.

Some of the rich men from New York and Virginia made fun of Jackson's clothes. They laughed at the way he wore his hair. A long pigtail tied with an eel-skin hung down his back. However, these men knew better than to laugh out loud. They had heard that Jackson had a hot temper.

When Jackson finished his work in Congress, he returned to Tennessee. He went back to being a lawyer. He also made a lot of money selling land.

Jackson was still interested in law. He became a judge. Many people said he was the best judge Tennessee had ever had. He also became major general of the Tennessee Militia. The Jacksons moved

Andrew Jackson's beloved
wife Rachel. Her happiest
days were spent at their
new home, The Hermitage.

into a new house with a lot of land. They called it
"The Hermitage."

Jackson grew cotton and raised horses. His favorite
horse was named Truxton. Truxton could run like
lightning. But there was another fast horse in
Tennessee. His name was Ploughboy.

Jackson and the man who owned Ploughboy
decided to race their horses.

Jackson spent the days before the race training
Truxton. One day Truxton hurt his leg. Jackson's
friends did not think Truxton had a chance to beat
Ploughboy. They begged Jackson not to let Truxton
race.

Jackson did not agree. He went up and patted

Truxton's nose. "You'll be all right, boy, won't you?" Jackson said.

Truxton seemed to understand. Jackson decided to let him race.

The day of the contest was cloudy. But hundreds of people came to the race track. The horse that won two out of three races would be the winner.

The first race began. Truxton got ahead of Ploughboy. His leg did not seem to bother him. The crowd cheered as Truxton won.

Then Truxton started limping. It did not seem possible that he could win the second race. Suddenly it started to rain. Perhaps the cool rain made the injured horse feel better. He went on to win the second race. That made it two out of three for Truxton.

Jackson was proud of him. And Rachel was proud of her husband. She knew that Jackson had given Truxton the will to win. In the future he would give many soldiers the will to win.

6. "Old Hickory"

Rachel and Andrew were happy at The Hermitage. Here they ran a large plantation and became known for their fine racing stable.

Although they did not have children of their own,

they raised several foster children and an adopted son, Andrew Jackson, Jr.

The news in the papers was exciting. England and France were at war. England needed every man she could get to help her fight.

English warships sometimes stopped American ships. The English took some of the American sailors to help them fight France. The English said the sailors on the American ships were really Englishmen.

The Americans were angry. America said England had no right to stop American ships at sea. Jackson still hated the English. He was glad when America declared war on England. The war is called the "War of 1812," for that was the year fighting began.

As major general of the Tennessee militia, Jackson ordered his men to get ready to fight. They met near Nashville. It was terribly cold. There was not enough firewood to keep them warm.

One man said Jackson was not a good general because his men almost froze.

"You scoundrel!" Jackson cried. "More of that talk and I'll ram a red-hot poker down your throat."

Jackson and his soldiers were sent to the Mississippi River. They were to rush to New Orleans if it were attacked. They camped by the river for a few weeks. Then they heard that the English were not ready to attack New Orleans.

Jackson and his soldiers started back to Nashville. The country was very wild. There were no roads and no bridges. Some of the soldiers were sick and could hardly walk. General Jackson seemed stronger than any of his men. Sometimes he ran back and forth trying to cheer them up.

One day Jackson ran past a group of soldiers. One of the soldiers said, "Just look at the general. He surely is tough!"

"You're right about that," another soldier said. "He's about as tough as . . ."

"What?" a third soldier asked.

"Hickory! That's the toughest thing I can think of, especially if the hickory is old."

"Old Hickory," the first soldier said. "That's a good nickname for General Jackson."

From that day on Jackson was known as "Old Hickory" to his soldiers.

7. War with the Indians

Jackson was not home long because soon there was trouble with the Indians. The Indians were angry because the pioneers had taken some of their land. They wanted to get it back.

A great Indian chief named Tecumseh had united many of the tribes to fight for their land. Tecumseh's followers were called "Red Sticks" because they had red war clubs.

One tribe of Indians that belonged to Tecumseh's Red Sticks was led by a chief named Red Eagle. He thought the Americans were too busy fighting the English to fight the Indians too. Red Eagle attacked Fort Mims, which was south of Tennessee. The Indians killed 250 Americans.

Jackson and his soldiers went after the Indians. There were several important battles which Jackson's men won. But each time, some Indians escaped to fight again. Red Eagle was always among them.

Red Eagle and his Indians lived in a village at Horseshoe Bend. It was protected on three sides by a river. The Indians built a wall out of logs on the fourth side. They cut holes in the wall to shoot through.

Jackson thought Red Eagle was at Horseshoe Bend. He was determined to catch him. So he and his men attacked the log wall. One soldier tried to climb it. The Indians killed him at once.

More soldiers rushed at the wall. Some were killed, but others got to the top. They dropped down on the far side. They fought the Indians with guns and swords.

The Indians had guns too, as well as bows and arrows and tomahawks. They fought fiercely. But

The Indian attack on Fort Mims (above) brought
Andrew Jackson and his men into battle against
Red Eagle and his Red Sticks.

slowly they were driven back toward the river. Many were killed.

Jackson sent a messenger to the Indians asking them to give up. The Indians shot at the messenger. So Jackson told his soldiers to fight harder.

Soon most of the Indians were killed or wounded. The few who were still alive hid in a small wooden fort. Jackson's soldiers used flaming arrows to set the fort on fire. The Indians came out and the battle was over.

However, Red Eagle had not been killed. He had not even been at Horseshoe Bend the day of the battle. Jackson was disappointed.

A few days later a man came to Jackson's camp. He did not have a gun or a bow and arrow. He looked thin and hungry.

"Who are you?" Jackson asked.

"I am Red Eagle," the man said in a tired vioce.

"You murderer!" Jackson cried. "You killed the women and children at Fort Mims."

"I have come to give myself up," Red Eagle said. "I am in your power."

"I ordered you brought to me in chains," Jackson said. "But you have come of your own free will."

"I have come to ask your help," Red Eagle said. "Not for myself. Not for my warriors. Most of them are dead."

"Then whom do you want me to help?" Jackson asked.

"The Indian women and children," Red Eagle said. "They have been driven into the woods with nothing to eat. They are starving."

"I will send help to your women and children," Jackson promised. He and Red Eagle shook hands.

"Go!" Jackson said. "Find your warriors who are still alive. Tell them to live in peace."

Red Eagle walked out of the camp. He never made trouble again.

8. The Battle of New Orleans

Jackson had made peace with the Indians. But war with England was still going on.

In May 1814, Jackson became a major general in the United States Army. He was placed in command of troops in Tennessee, Louisiana, and the Mississippi Territory.

Later that year, Jackson heard that the English planned to attack New Orleans at last. New Orleans was an important port near the mouth of the Mississippi River. Jackson rushed his army to New Orleans. He was worried. He knew the English had many more soldiers than he had.

There were some pirates living on an island south

Andrew Jackson, major general in the United States
Army and the defender of New Orleans

of New Orleans. Their leader was named Jean Lafitte. The English were trying to get Lafitte to fight on their side. They promised him a lot of money.

Jean Lafitte said "No." He wanted to help the Americans.

"I am the Lost Sheep," he wrote, "who desires to return to the flock."

At first Jackson said he would not take help from pirates. But he needed all the help he could get.

One dark night, Jean Lafitte came to see him. "Perhaps we are outlaws," the pirate said, "but we are Americans too. My men know the land south of New Orleans. They can help you beat the English."

"All right," Jackson said. "We will accept your help."

A few days later the English landed south of the city. There were several small battles. Slowly the English came closer and closer to New Orleans.

There was a canal between the English and the city. It ran from the Mississippi River to a swamp. Jackson's soldiers made a wall on their side of the canal. The English would have to climb over the wall to capture New Orleans. Jackson and his soldiers hid behind the wall, and waited.

One night Jackson's spies had very important news. The English were going to attack early the next morning.

"Get ready to fight," Jackson told his soldiers.

The soldiers near the swamp were knee-deep in mud and water. They were wet and cold.

Slowly, the sky grew light. But it was a foggy morning. The men could see only a little way.

Suddenly, the English sent up a rocket. Drops of fire fell in the fog.

Jackson knew it was a signal for the English to attack. He climbed on top of the wall and tried to see if the English were coming.

Just then a gust of wind blew the fog away. Jackson saw English soldiers marching toward the canal. Their white cross-belts stood out against their red coats.

"Pick your targets carefully," Jackson said, remembering his mother's advice. "Aim where the white belts cross, and you'll hit the English soldiers' hearts."

Cannon boomed and rifles crackled. The English

The Battle of New Orleans

soldiers started falling. The field was dotted with their red coats.

A few of the Englishmen got across the canal. They leaped upon the wall. It was no use. The Americans killed them or drove them back. The battle was soon over. The Americans had won.

Several weeks later, Jackson learned that the battle need not have been fought. A peace treaty had already been signed. But news traveled slowly in those days. Jackson and the English had no way of knowing that the war had ended.

The battle was still important. It made the English respect the United States Army, and it made Andrew Jackson a great American hero.

9. Fighting in Florida

Three years after the Battle of New Orleans, Jackson went to war again. This time he fought the Seminole Indians in Florida.

The Seminoles often crossed the United States border. They stole cattle and sometimes killed Americans. Florida belonged to Spain, but Spain did not have enough soldiers to punish the Indians.

Jackson marched his men into Florida. He heard that some Indians were at a Spanish fort in St. Marks, a town on the Gulf of Mexico.

When Jackson got to St. Marks, the Indians had fled. However, he did find an old Englishman named Arbuthnot.

"Have you helped the Indians?" Jackson asked.

"Yes," Arbuthnot admitted. "The English treated them badly, and you Americans rob them."

Jackson turned to one of his soldiers. "Arrest this man," he shouted. Arbuthnot was made a prisoner.

Then Jackson and his soldiers marched toward an Indian village on the Suwannee River. They hoped to capture the Seminoles there.

When they reached the Indian village, it was empty. The Indians had left. Jackson and his soldiers made camp. That night they captured an Englishman named Ambrister. He had a letter from Arbuthnot.

"The Americans are coming," the letter said. "Tell the Indians to hide."

Now Jackson knew why his long march had been useless. He arrested Ambrister and took him back to St. Marks. Jackson said that Ambrister and Arbuthnot were enemies of the United States. They should not have helped the Indians. He had the men tried. They were guilty. Ambrister was shot and Arbuthnot was hanged.

Jackson started out for Pensacola, the largest town in West Florida. He and his soldiers had to march through the swamps and wade across the rivers.

Some of the soldiers were barefoot when they reached Pensacola. The Spanish were afraid of them. They soon gave up. The Americans took Pensacola.

When the king of Spain heard what Jackson had done, he was angry. He said the United States must give Pensacola and St. Marks back to Spain. He wanted Jackson punished.

The two towns were given back to Spain. Then the United States offered five million dollars for all of Florida. Spain took it. Florida became United States territory. Jackson was not punished. He was sent back to Florida. He was the first American governor of the new territory.

10. Jackson Saves the Union

Jackson was governor of Florida for only a few months. Then he went to Washington as a senator from Tennessee.

At first Rachel stayed at The Hermitage. Jackson missed her, but he had many friends in the capital, and they invited him to dinners and parties. He soon became one of the most popular men in Washington. Many people said that Jackson should be president of the United States.

In 1824, he ran for president. He was defeated by John Quincy Adams. Adams was much better educated than Jackson, and his father, John Adams, had also been president.

Jackson ran for president again in 1828. Children sang that the election was between:

John Q. Adams who can write
And Andrew Jackson who can fight.

The people liked the man from the frontier who could fight. Jackson was elected.

He was the first president to come from one of the new states, west of the Appalachian mountains.

President-elect Andrew Jackson greeted the crowds that came to see him on his journey to Washington.

All the other presidents had come from either Massachusetts or Virginia. They had been born into rich families.

Jackson was the first president who had been born poor. His election proved that every boy had a chance to be president.

Before Jackson moved into the White House, Rachel became sick. She died just before Christmas.

Jackson was heartbroken. However, he was the new president. Rachel's niece, Emily, and her husband, Jack Donelson, moved into the White House with him. They had a little boy named Andrew Jackson Donelson. Their baby girl was born in the White House.

One day a man came to see the president on important business. But the business had to wait. The baby was asleep in the president's arms. Jackson did not want to wake her up.

He always liked children. "They are the only friends I have who do not pester me with advice," he once said.

Many grownups did pester him. Men who had voted for Jackson flocked to Washington. They wanted jobs.

"To the victors belong the spoils," these men said. "Fire the people who worked under Adams. Give us their jobs."

Jackson did fire many people. But he tried to be fair. Once a congressman asked him to fire an old man who had fought with George Washington. Jackson's blue eyes flashed with anger. "That old man has a pound of English bullets in his body. He keeps his job."

Other men came to see Jackson about more important matters. Congress had passed a law that South Carolina did not like. South Carolina said that if it did not like a law, it would not obey it.

Many people tried to tell Jackson what to do about South Carolina. Some thought South Carolina was right. Others were sure it was wrong. At first, Jackson would not say what he thought.

One night he went to a dinner party. He knew that what he said there would be in all the newspapers. He would tell the people what he thought. At the end of the dinner, Jackson asked the men to stand up. They would drink a toast together.

The President lifted his glass. He said, "Our Federal Union—it must be preserved!"

He meant that South Carolina did not have a right to disobey laws made by Congress. It it did, the United States might break up. Jackson thought the government in Washington was more important than the state government.

Later he said that South Carolina had better not

try fighting. If blood were shed, he promised to "hang the first man I lay my hands on . . . upon the first tree that I can reach."

Then Jackson asked Congress to give him the power to use the army and navy to enforce the law. South Carolina did not fight, so the army and navy were not needed. The Union was saved.

11. A Strong President

One afternoon Jackson went to see Charles Carroll. It was Charles Carroll's ninety-fourth birthday.

Charles Carroll was the only man still alive who had signed the Declaration of Independence. The old man was pleased that the president had come to see him. "I am honored," he said.

"No," Jackson said. "I am the one who is honored. When I was a boy I read the Declaration aloud. I read it to the farmers in South Carolina."

Charles Carroll's old eyes sparkled.

"There were some mighty big words in the Declaration of Independence," Jackson said with a smile. "It was hard for a little boy to read."

Charles Carroll laughed. "That was Thomas Jefferson's fault," he said. "He wrote it."

"By signing it you helped make America free," Jackson said, "and all America thanks you."

Jackson had three important ideas about America. He believed that all the people should take part in the government. He believed that all the states should stick together. And he believed that the president should have a great deal of power. These beliefs helped Jackson get elected a second time. In his second term he certainly needed power.

He was against the United States Bank. This was not really a government bank. It was a private bank owned mostly by rich men. The United States government kept its money in the bank. This helped the rich men get even richer.

"That's wrong," Jackson said. "The government's money should help all the people, not just those who are rich."

The men who ran the bank did not give in easily. One of them said, "Jackson may have killed Indians and Englishmen. But that does not mean he can kill our bank."

It was a hard fight. But Jackson finally won. The government's money went into state banks. This made it easier for ordinary people all over the country to borrow money.

Now Jackson's term in the White House was coming to an end. He did not run for president again. He helped his friend, Martin Van Buren, become the next president.

At The Hermitage Old Hickory returned to the life
of a country gentleman. His famous house is seen
in the background.

Jackson started on the long trip home. One night he stopped at a hotel. Some children came to his window and sang a song about him:

> *If I were President of these*
> *United States,*
> *I'd suck molasses candy and swing*
> *upon the gates.*
> *Oh, glory be to Jackson*
> *For he played many pranks,*
> *And glory be to Jackson*
> *For he blew up the banks.*

Jackson came to the window and waved.

He was happy when he reached The Hermitage. He ran the farm and wrote letters about government affairs.

In March 1845, Jackson learned that Florida had become a state. This meant that the United States flag would have 27 stars.

"Just think," Jackson said to a friend. "The stars in our flag have more than doubled since our country was founded."

But Jackson was a sick man. He died on June 8, 1845.

All over America the flag flew at half-mast. The nation was in mourning for Old Hickory.

Moving West

This story from Flatboat Days on Frontier Rivers *by James McCague tells about the dangers faced by pioneers on their way west in the late 1700s and early 1800s.*

Three heavily laden flatboats floated down the Ohio River one summer day in the year 1788. On board were several families from Virginia, with all of their household goods. They were settlers bound for new homes in the region known as Kentucky, which stretched along the south bank of the river.

On one of the boats was Parson Tucker, a young minister who had come along to start a church in the new settlement.

Dense forests covered both the riverbanks. In those early times few settlers lived there, but many Indian tribes did. Some of them were the enemies of all settlers. They knew from sad experience that white men always killed the deer and other game and took the best land for themselves.

But the folk on the three flatboats were strangers in this great wilderness. Though they had high hopes, none of them knew what really lay ahead of them. Perhaps young Parson Tucker was wondering about that as he gazed out over the broad river.

Then all of a sudden, a cry was heard from the north bank. A man had run out of the forest there. He waved his arms and screamed at the flatboats. As they drew nearer, the folk saw that he was a white man, and he was crying for help.

Quickly some of the men seized the oars and rowed their clumsy craft toward shore. It never occurred to them to pass the poor fellow by.

Too late, they saw that they had been tricked.

No sooner had the first two boats touched the bank than a horde of yelling Indians burst out of the woods. A shower of arrows struck down many of the settlers. The rest, taken by surprise, had no chance to defend themselves.

Shrill war cries split the air. Stabbing and hacking with knives and tomahawks, the braves swarmed up over the flatboats' sides. In a few minutes every person on both boats was killed.

The third flatboat, lagging a little way behind the others, had not yet reached the shore. Some of the men on board tried to row away. Others had time to snatch up their flintlock rifles as the Indians came splashing through the shallow water to attack them too.

They fired one hasty volley. Then, using the long rifles as clubs, they beat the braves back. But there were too many Indians. They kept on attacking. One by one, the white men went down in fierce, hand-to-hand fighting. At last the flatboat drifted out into deep water again.

Now only one of the men on board was left alive. He was Parson Tucker. He was bleeding from many wounds, and the battle was not yet over.

Several braves dragged a canoe from its hiding place among some reeds on the riverbank. Leaping into it, they paddled swiftly after the flatboat.

The women on the boat were as brave and hardy as their husbands had been.

One woman picked up an empty rifle lying on the deck. She tore the powder horn and bullet pouch from a dead man's body. Quickly she poured a big charge of gunpowder down the rifle barrel. With the long ramrod she rammed a bullet down on top of it. Then she rammed in a patch of greased cloth to hold the bullet in place.

But all this took time. The speedy canoe was drawing closer. Coolly the woman cocked the rifle and handed it to Parson Tucker. In spite of his wounds, he stood up and took careful aim.

Bang! A brave yelled in pain and fell out of the canoe.

Other women were loading rifles also. They passed them to Parson Tucker, each in turn. He was a good shot. Every bullet hit its mark. Soon only a few Indians were left alive in the canoe. They had had enough. Turning away, they paddled back to shore as fast as they could go.

Thankfully, some of the women bandaged the young preacher's wounds. The rest took hold of the long, heavy oars and rowed the flatboat down the river as best they could. After a while they managed to reach Limestone, a small settlement on the Kentucky shore. Then at last they were safe. But Parson Tucker was so badly hurt that he died a few days later.

In spite of the dangers and the hardships, more and more such settlers came floating down the Ohio River every year. America was a young, growing nation. Americans were pushing westward, seeking new land and new opportunities.

The great, broad river was a natural roadway for them to follow. Nothing could stop them.

People like the settlers with Parson Tucker were called emigrants. Many of them had come a long way before they ever reached the Ohio River.

They had trudged over rough, stony roads through the Allegheny Mountains, with their belongings piled in wagons or on the backs of pack horses. Boys and girls had walked beside their mothers and fathers. Most families had driven their cows, pigs, and other farm animals along with them.

Some of these people came from eastern Pennsylvania. Some came from Maryland, Virginia, or other states along the shores of the Atlantic Ocean. Nearly all of them headed for the town of Pittsburgh, in western Pennsylvania.

The first thing that weary emigrants looked for when they got to town was a place to stay. Then they hurried out to see about buying a flatboat.

The flatboat was the family home—maybe the home of more than one family—for the long trip down the Ohio River. She was not a pretty craft, but she was roomy. And if the workmen had done their jobs well, she was good and sturdy.

Under the low roof were stowed all of the things the emigrants would need. Each family was sure to have brought a plow, some pots and kettles, an ax, a grindstone, and maybe a spinning wheel. There were warm blankets and quilts, several sides of bacon, and a few bags of flour or cornmeal.

Of course the men had their rifles, a supply of gunpowder, and some bars of lead to be melted down and made into bullets.

In whatever space was left, the families would live and sleep and eat their meals. The women cooked over a fire in a box full of sand, with a stovepipe sticking up through the roof to carry off the smoke. We must not forget the animals. They went along too.

One man who traveled down the Ohio in 1815 was reminded of Noah's Ark by some of the flatboats he saw. In a book he wrote, he told of "old and young, servants, cattle, hogs, sheep, fowls, and animals of all kinds . . . all embarked and floating down on the same bottom."

Like Noah and his family in the Bible, most of the emigrants finally came safely to land.

Often they simply ran their flatboats onto the shore and went on living in them while they chopped down trees, plowed the earth, and planted crops. Then they took the boats apart and used the planks and beams in the cabins they built. They were no longer flatboat folk; they were farmers.

James McCague

DAVY CROCKETT
(1786–1836)

—the beloved folk hero of the American
frontier—grew up in eastern Tennessee
in his father's country tavern. Young
Davy worked hard for neighboring
settlers to earn enough money to pay
off his father's debts. There was little
time for schooling. Later, when Davy
married, he tried his hand at farming,
but he was always happier in the woods
hunting wild animals and exploring the
wilderness. Davy moved with his family
to frontier country in western Tennessee
and soon went off to fight the Creek
Indians under Andrew Jackson. He
became a justice of the peace, a colonel
in the militia, and a member of the
Tennessee state legislature. His honesty
and independence—and the tales he
told about his adventures in the woods—
endeared him to the people, and he was
elected to Congress from Tennessee. In
1835, Davy moved on to Texas, where
he died in the heroic defense of the
Alamo. It was his last frontier.

Davy Crockett
Hero of the Wild Frontier
by Elizabeth R. Moseley

1. Davy

As soon as his chores were done, Davy Crockett ran off to the woods. Stepping light-footed as a deer, he followed a trail to the edge of the forest.

The nine-year-old boy hid behind a bush and sat very still. He was watching a mother bird. She was busy gathering her young ones under her wings before dark.

Davy lived in eastern Tennessee. His father had a tavern on the trail between Knoxville and Abingdon, Virginia. In 1795 the land there was still almost wilderness. There were only a few close neighbors and no schools.

John Crockett and his wife Rebecca were very poor. They tried hard to make a living for their six boys and three girls. But paying guests at the tavern were few and far between.

Suddenly a loud clear call rang out through the woods. "Da-a-vy! Da-a-vy! Come to supper!" called his mother.

The mother quail fluttered in alarm. Davy sat still. He whispered softly, "Yes, ma'am. I'm a-coming."

The young quail ran swiftly to their mother and nestled beside her.

"Davy Crockett! You come here this very instant!"

Again Davy answered her in a soft whisper, "Yes, ma'am. I'm a-coming."

Rebecca Crockett stood for a moment at the door. Then she returned to the table.

"That's the second time I've called that boy," she told her husband. "Davy would live in the woods if he could."

Just then Davy stepped through the door.

"Why didn't you answer your ma, Davy?"

"I answered, pa."

"Did anyone hear Davy's answer?"

The young Crocketts solemnly shook their heads and looked at their plates.

"About how loud was your answer?"

Davy glanced quickly at his older brothers. They continued to pay close attention to their plates. With a sheepish look, the boy faced his father.

"Not very loud, pa," he said. "I was watching some quail, and I didn't want to scare them."

"Humph! These woods still have a few Indians in them. Eighteen years ago they killed my ma and pa right in their own cabin. When we call you, it might mean life or death. Is that clear?"

Davy nodded.

"And another thing, Davy, when you answered your ma, you knew that she couldn't hear you. Yet you told me you answered. That wasn't honest. Don't ever do that again."

"I won't, pa."

"Now eat your supper. Some drovers will be here soon. They're driving their cattle to Virginia. You boys must be ready to bed down the herd."

Davy sat down beside his sister Jane. "Janie, do you know what I did while I watched the quail?"

"No. What?"

"Practiced grinning," Davy said with a big smile.

"What for, Davy?"

"I'm going to out-grin a possum someday. He'll fall right down out of the tree, plumb dead. All I'll have to do is pick him up and bring him home."

Janie giggled. Davy always had a funny story to tell.

2. Davy Goes A-Traveling

"Huh-ee! Huh-ee! Get back there, you crazy old cow!" Davy was helping a man with his cattle.

Jacob Siler had stopped at Crockett's Tavern. He was a drover, who bought cattle in the backwoods and drove them to Virginia to sell. He was finding it hard to manage the herd alone, and he was still 400 miles from home.

The drover watched Davy as he worked. He saw that the boy was quick and cheerful.

"John," he said to Mr. Crockett, "would you consider hiring out Davy to me for the rest of this drive?"

"The boy is only twelve years old, Jacob."

"But he's a pretty good worker. I'll send him back as soon as I deliver this herd."

Money was scarce in the Crockett household, and boys were not. So Mr. Crockett agreed to hire out Davy.

Before Davy left home, his mother made him a new coonskin cap. His father gave him a rifle.

"There may be times on the trail when you'll need this, Davy," his father said. "You probably won't meet any unfriendly Indians, but you might want a rabbit or a squirrel for supper."

Davy lived, as a child, in the small country inn owned by his father, John Crockett.

Davy was thrilled. "I reckon it'll come in right handy." He patted his gun proudly.

"Remember, Davy, you're only bound out to Jacob Siler for the cattle drive. Come back home as soon as you can find someone coming this way."

Poor men often hired out a child to work for another family until grown. Davy was glad he was coming home when the drive was over.

At the end of the journey, Siler paid Davy six dollars. "Now you're to help me on the farm, Davy," he said.

"But pa told me I was to come home."

"Maybe he changed his mind, boy."

Davy did not know what to believe. But he had to obey the man.

Mr. Siler kept Davy very busy. He was not really unkind, but the boy was unhappy.

One Sunday, three wagons passed along the road near the Silers' house. Davy saw a neighbor from Tennessee. His name was Dunn, and he lived near Crockett's Tavern.

Davy ran into the road and waved his arms wildly. Mr. Dunn stopped his team. The boy scrambled up onto the wagon.

"Davy Crockett! Where did you come from?"

Quickly Davy explained. "Can you help me, sir? I want to go home."

Mr. Dunn scratched his head. "Davy, are you sure

Siler promised to send you home at the end of the drive?"

"Yes, sir. I heard him." Tears filled Davy's eyes.

"Well, boy," said Mr. Dunn with a wink, "we're going to spend the night at the next tavern. It's about seven miles down the road. We'll be on our way again at daybreak. I could just happen to find you in one of the wagons after we're well on the way."

Davy jumped down from the wagon and ran to the Silers' house to complete his chores. After supper he got ready for bed.

Mr. Siler was in the living room. He saw Davy start upstairs.

"Why are you going to bed so early, Davy?" Mr. Siler said. "We can't work tomorrow. It's snowing hard."

Davy yawned. "I'm sleepy, sir. I think I'll turn in."

The boy lay quiet as a mouse long after the others went to bed. Then he took his clothes, which he had made into a bundle. Silently he crept down the stairs. Every step made a creaking noise. His heart beat fast. Finally he reached the yard safely.

The snow was almost up to his knees, but the homesick boy trudged down the road. He was almost frozen when he reached the tavern where Mr. Dunn was staying. The next morning the wagon had another passenger.

Davy was on his way home at last.

3. A Short School Term

Davy looked longingly at the bright autumn woods. They seemed to be calling him. He wished he were going hunting. Instead, he was going to school.

More people had settled near Crockett's Tavern. A man named Benjamin Kitchen had started a school. John Crockett had enrolled his children.

Davy was the biggest boy who could not read or write. His brothers had learned while he was in Virginia.

One morning as he read aloud from the first reader, he heard a snicker behind him. He looked around and saw a tall teenager named Johnny Crawford making fun of him.

"Don't mind Johnny," Davy's neighbor whispered. "Everybody knows he is a bully. He picks on all the boys smaller than he is."

Davy frowned. "I'll get even with Johnny Crawford if it's the last thing I do," he decided.

Before classes were over, Davy left the schoolroom. He hurried along the path that led to Johnny's home. About a half mile from the Crawford house, he hid in the bushes.

When Johnny came walking by, Davy jumped out and stood before him. Johnny was really a coward. He started to run. Davy caught him, and the battle was on.

Davy attended a frontier school much like this one.

Both boys were bruised and bleeding when it ended. Davy had won.

"Don't you ever bully smaller boys again. If you have to fight, pick on somebody your size. Hear me?"

"I promise I won't pick on anyone," blubbered Johnny.

Davy dusted his clothes, picked up his books, and started home.

The next morning, he stared at his face in the mirror. Davy knew that Johnny's face looked worse than his. The teacher would surely punish them both for fighting. Mr. Kitchen kept a hickory stick by his desk. He whipped the boys who caused trouble.

On the way to school, Davy stopped. "You go on," he told his brothers. "I think I'd better stay away from school for a few days. When Mr. Kitchen sees Johnny's black eye, he'll be angry. I'll meet you here after school. Then pa won't know that I've been in the woods all day."

For four days, Davy roamed in his beloved woods. He could not use his gun. The shots would be heard at home. But he checked the traps that he and his brothers had set.

The teacher thought Davy was sick. His father thought he was in school. On the fourth day, the two men met.

"When will Davy be back in school?" asked the teacher.

"Hasn't he been in school?" Mr. Crockett said.

Mr. Kitchen shook his head. "Not for four days."

"H'm! I didn't know that. I'll look into it."

That evening when Davy finished his chores, his father was waiting for him.

"Your teacher tells me you haven't been in school. Where have you been?"

"Pa, I had a fight on the way home from school. I thought I had better let Mr. Kitchen cool off before I went back. He's pretty handy with a hickory stick."

"Fighting, huh? Well, I'm right handy with a hickory stick myself."

Mr. Crockett was angry. Davy saw that he was holding a stick in his hand. The boy turned and took to his heels with his father behind him. But Davy soon outran him. He hid in the woods. Finally, his father gave up the chase.

"If I go home, pa will whip me," thought Davy. "If I go to school, I'll get another whipping from Mr. Kitchen. What shall I do?"

Then he remembered that a neighbor was leaving for Virginia the next day. He was taking some cattle there. Maybe he would need a helper. With that in mind, Davy lay down on a bed of pine needles and went to sleep.

The neighbor was glad to have a helper. Soon Davy was on the road. He felt much safer as the distance widened between him and his father and his teacher.

At the end of the drive, Davy was paid four dollars. He tucked the money into his pocket. Then he made a decision. He would stay in Virginia and work until his father's temper had cooled.

For several years, Davy supported himself by working at odd jobs. Just before his sixteenth birthday, he could stand it no longer. He was so homesick that he returned to Tennessee.

"Did you walk all the way home, Davy?" asked Janie.

"Of course not," said Davy with a smile. "I just latched on to the tail of a kite and sailed in."

4. Farmer and Hunter

Davy was happy to be home. And his father seemed glad to have him back with the family once more.

One day Mr. Crockett talked to Davy, "Son, do you remember what I said when I hired you out to Jacob Siler for that wagon drive? I said I'd never hire you out again. But I just don't seem to be able to stay out of debt. Now that your two older brothers are married, they can't help me anymore. The truth of the matter is, I owe Abe Wilson $35.00. He wants you to work for him six months to pay it. Will you do it?"

"Sure I will, pa. I'll be glad to help you."

Davy went to work at once. When the six months ended, he asked a neighbor for a job on his farm.

"Davy, everybody around here knows you're honest and a good worker. I certainly could use you. But did you know your pa owes me $40.00?"

"No, sir. I didn't."

"I tell you what I'll do. If you will work six months to pay off his debt, I'll give you a regular job."

Davy agreed to work for the man. At the end of six months, he told his father the debt was paid. Crockett looked at his son with tears in his eyes.

"Davy, this makes me mighty proud. I reckon I just don't have the knack of saving money."

One day a beautiful girl came to visit the neighbor's

There were trees to fell, fences to put up, and houses to build on frontier farms. Davy worked for a time for other settlers in order to help his father pay his debts.

family. Seventeen-year-old Davy fell in love with her. Soon he asked her to marry him.

"No, Davy," she replied. "I like you, but I'm going to marry someone else. He is a schoolteacher. I gave him my promise, and I won't break it."

Davy was heartbroken. He thought he had been refused because he could not read and write. The time had come to do something about it.

The first thing Davy did was to ask his boss for help.

"One of my sons is a teacher. He will help you. Work for him two days each week, and he'll give you lessons."

For several months, Davy worked hard at his lessons. He made rapid progress because he wanted to learn.

Soon he met another girl, who made him forget his first love. Her name was Mary Finley. Polly, as she was called, was a pretty, blue-eyed Irish girl. Davy told his family that she was sweeter than sugar.

Davy and Polly were married in August 1806. Their wedding presents were a spinning wheel and two cows and calves. The happy young couple rented a little farm.

Davy worked hard at farming. But hunting was his great love. He was a skilled woodsman, and his family always had plenty of game to eat.

Nothing was more exciting to Davy than a bear hunt. He would go through the forests watching for a hollow tree. Davy would walk slowly around the tree looking for bear signs. If the bark had short scratches, a bear was likely to be sleeping inside. When the scratches were long, the bear had slipped down the tree trunk and moved on.

If the bear were still there, Davy's hounds would race around the tree, barking furiously. The bear would climb down snarling and growling. Then Davy would call his dogs away and take careful aim at the great beast.

Grizzly bears are very powerful and dangerous animals. Sometimes they claw hunting dogs to death. If Davy were not careful, he could be killed too. But Davy was a fine shot. He seldom missed. He called his trusty rifle Old Betsy.

Polly was always happy when Davy returned home safely. Two sons were born while the Crocketts lived in eastern Tennessee. Their names were John and William.

Before long Davy began to get restless. He complained of having to pay high rent for his farm. Deer and small game were still plentiful, but bears were getting scarce. Worst of all, too many people had moved into the area. Davy felt crowded. In the summer of 1811, he made up his mind to leave.

"Polly, pack up the boys," he said. "We're going to go west."

Before the end of September, the Crocketts were on their way to middle Tennessee. After two years, they moved again. Their new home was a few miles north of the Alabama line. West of Alabama was Mississippi Territory. It was still largely Indian country.

Soon a corn patch was planted. Wood was stacked beside the cabin wall. Meat was plentiful. Davy had a pile of skins ready to trade at the settlement for supplies like salt, sugar, flour, and tea. Polly and the boys were happy in their snug little home.

5. War with the Red Sticks

"I'm a-going to join the militia and get after those murdering Red Sticks," Davy told his wife. "They sure murdered a bunch of people down at Fort Mims."

Tecumseh, a Shawnee chief, had united many of the Indian tribes in the area. He was trying to stop the white people from moving into the Mississippi Territory. Indian warriors who followed the mighty Tecumseh painted their war clubs red. For this reason they were called the "Red Sticks."

The Red Sticks, under the great Creek chief, Red Eagle, had attacked Fort Mims, on the lower Alabama River. They killed hundreds of men, women, and children. Now Red Eagle and his braves were moving north.

"If we don't stop them, they'll soon find their way up here," said Davy.

Davy's wife hated to have him go. But she knew he had to. Soon she was packing his saddle bags and filling his powder horn.

Many Tennessee men soon joined the militia. They served under the famous Indian fighter, Andrew Jackson.

Because he was a fine woodsman, Davy was assigned to a scouting party. These men were sent to find out where the Indians were and what they were doing. The silent, swift-footed Creeks were not easy to follow in the woods. But the scouts had learned to move silently and swiftly too.

One night Davy and his partner were returning late

After the massacre at Fort Mims, Davy joined Jackson's forces in fighting the Red Sticks.

to camp. Suddenly they saw some Red Sticks hiding their canoes around the bend of the river. From behind a tree, Davy watched them. The Indians started to creep through the woods to attack the soldiers.

Davy sent his partner to warn the men in camp. Then he slipped past the Indians. He moved their canoes and hid them without making a sound.

Just as the Indians were about to attack the camp, Davy gave a loud and fearsome yell. All the soldiers joined in. The woods rang with the uproar. The Red Sticks, frightened by the strange noise, turned and ran to the river. Their canoes had disappeared! When Davy gave another terrifying yell, the Indians leaped into the river and escaped.

Davy served the army well. But he was happy when he could return home.

Early in 1815, a little girl was born to the Crocketts. She was called Polly.

Six months later Mrs. Crockett died after a short illness. At first Davy and his children tried to manage without help. Then Davy asked his youngest brother and his wife to come and stay. This did not work out. So Davy began to look around for a new wife.

Soon he married Elizabeth Patton, a widow with two young children. She was a strong and sensible woman. Her husband had been killed in the war with the Red Sticks.

On the wedding day, the guests were all gathered in Elizabeth's living room waiting for the bride to appear. Davy and the minister stood, ready for the ceremony to start. Suddenly the sound of pigs was heard. Through the doorway waddled a big fat pig, grunting every step of the way. Everyone burst into laughter. Davy quickly guided the fat uninvited visitor back through the door. He said, "Old Hook, from now on I'll do the grunting around here!"

People in large numbers were coming to middle Tennessee. The woods Davy loved were being settled.

In 1817 Davy took Elizabeth and their children to Lawrence County, about 80 miles away. He opened two mills at the head of Shoal Creek. One was a powder mill, and here he made gunpowder. The other was a grist mill, where grain was ground into meal or flour. Things were going well for Davy and his family.

6. Running for the Legislature

There were thick patches of tall, woody reeds growing in the Tennessee frontierland known as canebrakes. Often the canes were six or seven feet tall.

One morning Davy and his oldest son, with their dogs, tracked a big bear into a canebrake. Vines and briers grew around the cane stalks. Walking was very painful.

Davy Crockett. The buckskin-clad frontiersman became a colonel in the militia, a town commissioner, and then a member of the Tennessee state legislature.

Finally Davy got close enough to get a shot at the big beast. But Davy was hot and tired. He found it hard to hold Old Betsy steady. Crack! The bullet crashed into the bear's shoulder. The animal turned and started moving toward him. Davy reached for his hunting knife. It was gone! He must have lost it in the thick cane. Quickly he began to reload.

Just before the bear reached him, Davy raised Old Betsy again. This time his aim was true. The bear fell just a few feet away.

Davy and his son found the hunting knife, skinned the bear, and took the meat home.

The name and fame of Davy Crockett spread over the whole Tennessee frontier. Besides being a skilled woodsman, he was also known to be honest and dependable. The people of Lawrence County not only trusted him, but liked him as well.

Each county had its own company of militia. These soldiers were called upon in cases of emergency. Davy became a colonel in the militia in 1818.

Later he was elected to be justice of the peace. After that, he became town commissioner of Lawrenceburg. This was something like being town manager. As the little town grew, there were many records to be kept. Davy now had use for his training in reading, writing, and arithmetic.

In 1821 he became a candidate for the Tennessee legislature. People flocked to hear his speeches. They loved the funny stories he mixed in with his remarks about politics. Davy told about his trained bear, Death Hug, and his pet alligator, Old Mississippi. These were imaginary animals to which he gave human abilities.

"Gentlemen," Davy said, "you ought to see Death Hug sit at the table. He eats just like a man. When he can find his glasses, he likes to read. But he's careless with those glasses. They're always getting lost."

"Old Mississippi comes in handy when I don't have a horse," he went on. "After a hard day of hunting, I just get on that old alligator and ride home fast."

"I hear you're a pretty good shot, Davy," someone in the audience shouted.

"You must be right," Davy said. "Just the other day I was walking through the woods. I spied a raccoon a-sittin' on a limb. I lifted Old Betsy and drew a bead on that creature. What do you think happened? That old coon raised his paw and said, 'Are you Davy Crockett?' I nodded. 'Well, don't shoot,' he said. 'I'll come down.' Now gentlemen, I'm a modest man. When he gave up so quickly, I was embarrassed."

After Davy was elected to the legislature, he began to be uneasy.

"I don't know a thing about lawmaking," he said to his wife. "What will I do when I get to the legislature?"

"Don't worry," replied Elizabeth. "Just remember to follow your own advice, 'Be sure you're right, then go ahead.'"

7. A Gentleman from the Cane

Colonel Davy Crockett was present in September 1821, when the Tennessee legislature met. He had two major interests. One was to see that the poor people of west Tennessee had a chance to buy the land they had cleared. The other was to get the boundaries set on this land.

Davy was dressed in deerskin jacket and pants and

wore his coonskin cap. He looked different from the other legislators.

Early in the session, he made his first speech. When he finished, a member who disagreed with him arose. This man was dressed in the height of fashion. He wore white ruffles on his shirt front and at his cuffs.

"You have heard the opinion of the gentleman from the cane," he said with a smile and a nod toward Colonel Crockett. A wave of laughter swept through the room.

Davy sat quietly until the man finished his speech. But he decided to give the man a lesson in manners. That afternoon he found a piece of white ruffling. It was much like that on the rude man's shirt. The next day most of the members were in their seats when Davy rose to speak again.

Pinned to the front of his deerskin jacket was the white ruffle. Before he could open his mouth, the members saw the ruffle. They burst into laughter, rose to their feet, and clapped and shouted. Without saying a word, Colonel Crockett had won their respect and admiration.

When Davy returned home from this session of the legislature, he found his family worried and upset. Both mills had been swept away by a flash flood.

"Don't worry," he said, sweeping his little daughter up in his arms. "I've decided to sell this place. We'll move to the Obion River country. It's about 150 miles from here—farther west, of course. We ought to be able to have our new cabin ready by the time the next session of the legislature is over."

"Pa, are there any Indians in the Obion River country?" asked Robert.

Davy nodded. "Yes, son. There are some Chickasaws living around there, but they're friendly."

Mrs. Crockett sighed with relief. "I'm glad to hear they're friendly. I can look out for panthers and black bears. But I am mortally scared of unfriendly Indians."

"How many bears did you kill last year, pa?" asked Robert.

"Well, son, if my count was right, I killed 105. That was 58 in the fall and winter and 47 in the spring. Along with the buffalo and deer meat, that gave us plenty to eat, didn't it?"

As the children grew older, Davy needed more money. When he was home from the legislature, he decided to make barrel staves. He had to build barges to carry the staves down the Mississippi River to New Orleans. There was a good market in the busy seaport for the staves.

He hired men to help him cut down trees and saw them into barrel staves. Then he loaded them on the barges.

Davy took his staves down the Mississippi on
barges manned by rivermen. Many of the stories
Davy later told of river life may have been based
on the tales he heard on this trip.

Piloting on the Mississippi River was a difficult job. Davy did not know it, but he had hired a pilot who was not familiar with the dangers of the river. A few miles from Memphis, all three barges went out of control and began to sink. All the men swam to safety but Davy. He was caught in a hole in the deck of the barge.

He was about to drown when two of his men saw what had happened. They returned and pulled him loose. Although he had lost a lot of money, he was happy to be alive.

His family was glad when he arrived home. Robert said, "Pa, we heard you came out of that old river just as dry as a bone. Is that true?"

With his usual courage when faced with trouble, Davy gave a big smile. "Why, of course it's true, boy," he said. "Don't you know I can run faster, dive deeper, stay under longer, and come up drier than any man in the whole of creation?"

8. Colonel Crockett Goes to Congress

Davy made many friends in the state legislature. He did not hesitate to fight for what he thought was right. The people of west Tennessee liked him. After a time, they began to ask him to run for the United States Congress.

"Shucks," Davy said, "I'm not the man for that. I know nothing about national matters."

His friends continued to ask him. At last he agreed to run. But not enough time was left for his political campaign. In August 1825, he was defeated. He began at once to work for the next election.

His opponent for congressman from Tennessee was a skillful politician. He decided to ignore Davy. The name of Davy Crockett was never mentioned in any of his speeches.

One day the two men spoke at the same meeting. It was warm, and the meeting was held out of doors.

Davy's opponent thundered and roared with big words and big promises. "You are my people," he said. "And I know when you go to the polls, you will vote for me."

In a nearby field was a flock of guinea hens.

"Pot-rack! Pot-rack! Pot-rack!" the birds called.

The loud sound of the guineas filled the air. They had wandered close to the stand and were frightened. Their clatter made it impossible for the speaker to be heard. He sat down.

When all was quiet again, Davy came forward to speak.

"I'm glad my friend here understands guinea talk," he said with a bow to his opponent. "He ignored my presence so long that everybody got tired listening to him. But it took my fine feathered friends to tell him. Those guineas made it mighty plain. They were saying, 'Crockett! Crockett! Crockett!'"

The audience laughed and shouted for more. When election day arrived, Davy Crockett was elected.

In December 1827, Davy went to Washington. Although he dressed like everyone else in Congress, he talked like the frontiersman that he was. His clear thinking, his keen mind, and his ready wit were soon recognized. He knew that he did not know about "Congress matters." But he listened carefully, and he learned from what he heard.

The next year Tennessee's Andrew Jackson was elected president of the United States. At the end of the war with the Red Sticks, General Jackson had held a conference with the Creek Indian chiefs.

"You must sign a treaty," the tall general had told them. "You must give half of all your lands to the United States government. We promise that your people may keep the other half as long as they live."

The Indian chiefs were not happy, but they had signed the treaty. Now, fifteen years later, President Jackson wanted the Indians to give up all their land and move across the Mississippi.

When Davy heard this, he was angry. "Whoever heard of that way of doing things? That land belongs to the Indians. I'll fight to help them keep it."

"I don't think you should, Davy," a friend said. "Jackson won't like it."

"I don't care. It's not right. I'll fight it with every breath in my body."

"You may not be reelected if you do," his friend warned.

"That'll be all right with me. I can always go back to hunting bears."

Davy worked hard to keep the Indians from being moved. But Congress passed the bill. The Indians were forced to set out for their new homes.

Davy had liked Andrew Jackson when Jackson was his army commander. But Davy could no longer be his friend. He could not forgive Jackson for forcing the Indians from their land. Davy spoke his mind freely. By doing so, he lost many votes when he ran for his fourth term in Congress. He was not reelected.

In spite of his disappointment, Davy continued to live by his motto, "Be sure you're right, then go ahead!"

9. "Remember the Alamo!"

Davy did return to Congress to finish his term. But when it came to an end in 1835, he was tired of politics.

"I've been knocked down and dragged out," Davy said. "Now I'm done with politics for the present. I'm going to Texas!"

Davy Crockett was a frontiersman. The frontier was moving west, and he wanted to move with it.

Texas was owned by Mexico. Since 1821, the Mexicans had granted land to Americans. Now there were about 30,000 Americans living in Texas.

Davy traveled to Texas with some friends. The Red River Valley in east Texas delighted him. Right away he made up his mind to settle there. The fields were rich and green. There was plenty of timber, and the water was sparkling clear and cold. Buffalo passed through going north or south as the seasons changed.

"Texas is the garden spot of the world," Davy wrote to his daughter. "It has the best land and prospects for health I ever saw. It's worth a fortune to any man to come here. There is a world of country to settle."

Davy planned to move his family to Texas. He felt that trouble was brewing in the big territory, but he was looking to the future. He took the oath of allegiance to the Texas government and joined the volunteer militia. This would allow him to vote and hold office.

Mexico was too busy with revolutions to manage the Texas lands. But in the early 1830s it tried to strengthen its rule over the settlers. It also tried to stop more United States settlers from coming in. The Texans rebelled. They wanted their independence.

Santa Anna, the new president of Mexico, decided

to punish them. With nearly 3,000 men, he marched toward San Antonio. Davy heard the bad news.

"That's where that little fort is, isn't it?" he said to one of his friends.

"Yes," the friend replied. "The fort is called the Alamo. It used to be a Spanish mission. Colonel Jim Bowie has gone to help the men there. But they need more help badly."

"What are we waiting for?" said Davy.

A small party was soon on its way. The men reached the Alamo in February. Inside the fort, they found about 150 men in good spirits. They were all determined to fight for "liberty or death." Colonel William Travis was in command. He assigned each man to a special place. All hope of further help had gone.

"Colonel Bowie, have you got that rib-tickler of yours ready?" Davy asked. "You could tickle a fellow's ribs right smart with that without making him laugh."

Bowie grinned. He knew Davy was referring to the knife that he had designed. He used it for skinning bears.

"It's ready, Colonel Crockett," Bowie said. "Now when are those Mexicans going to show themselves?"

The words were hardly out of his mouth when the shout rang out, "Here they come! To your stations!"

The men rushed to their places. Blasts from the cannon filled the air.

Davy Crockett, fighting bravely with Old Betsy in
his hand, died defending the Alamo.

"Show your faces so Old Betsy and me can get a bead on you," shouted Davy.

Old Betsy was soon hitting her targets. But Davy and the men in the Alamo were greatly outnumbered. Santa Anna's men swept into the fort. On they came, past the stacked mattresses and sandbags that sheltered the brave defenders. Their bayonets were drawn. Bodies were tossed aside like so much straw. The mass slaughter was watched by each man until it reached him.

Davy Crockett and Jim Bowie, with all the others, fought on bravely until the last man fell.

Davy lay dead, Old Betsy by his side. But Davy had not died in vain.

"Remember the Alamo!" became the cry that rallied and united the Americans in Texas. General Sam Houston and his men defeated the Mexicans, and Santa Anna was taken prisoner. The Texas that Davy had come to love became a republic. Later it would become part of the United States.

Davy had fought and died to make it all come true. It was his last frontier.

Vol. I. "*Go Ahead!*" No. 3.

Davy Crockett's
18 ALMANACK, 37
OF WILD SPORTS IN THE WEST,
Life in the Backwoods, & Sketches of Texas.

O KENTUCKY! THE HUNTERS OF KENTUCKY!!!

Nashville, Tennessee. Published by the heirs of Col. Crockett.

Colonel Crockett's "Riproarious" Frontier

There was the real Davy Crockett—sturdy hunter, farmer, congressman, and hero of the Alamo. And then there was the comic Colonel Crockett of *Davy Crockett's Almanacks*! This bigger-than-life hero of the wild frontier, based on the real Davy, swaggered through strange and marvelous adventures. The colonel and his friends and relatives outwitted man and beast and won every battle against impossible odds!

Davy Crockett's Almanacks were published from 1835 to 1856, first by the real Davy Crockett and then, after his death at the Alamo, by others. The *Almanacks* told farmers what kind of weather they could expect in the coming year. But more than that, they were a source of entertainment. Frontier folks roared at the funny pictures and tall tales that were included in each issue. The stories were read and reread and then told over and over again during the long, bitter winters. The folks on Colonel Crockett's imaginary frontier were a lot more fun than the plain, everyday folks on the real frontier!

There was Nance Bowers, who "could outscream a thunderbolt or a dozen wildcats and wiped her feet with her hair"; Mike Fink, "the celebrated Mississippi roarer, snag-lifter, and flatboat skuller"; Davy's sailor friend Ben Hardin, who "could catch a whale by the throat and squeeze or flog several casks of oil out of him"; and Davy himself, who could "run faster, jump higher, squat lower, dive deeper, stay under longer, and come out drier than any man in the country."

Some of Davy's friends and their adventures are pictured in the following pages. They were "ring-tailed roarers" all!

Mike Fink

"Ring-tailed roarers" Mike Fink (left) and Davy Crockett (right). Below, Ben Hardin waves Davy's flag triumphantly as Davy and his pet bear Death Hug row faster than a Mississippi River steamboat.

Davy Crockett

Death Hug   Ben Hardin   Davy Crockett

FRONTIER FUN

On Colonel Crockett's frontier, man met beast and usually came out on top! Treed by a bear, this backwoods hero is about to turn his enemy into "bar meat" steaks. Below, a brave woodsman runs off with the rattles of a "slippery-slimy critter" of the forest.

Frontier women were a hardy lot too! Oak Wing's sister was followed one day by a bear who was interested in sampling the sausages she was carrying. The scrappy lady grabbed the scruff of the bear's neck in her teeth and pulled as hard as she could. The bear pulled as hard as *he* could too! Before long that bear's skin had come clean off, leaving him "as naked as he was born!" That winter Oak Wing's sister had a nice warm petticoat, made out of the "pesky varmint's" hide.

SAM HOUSTON
(1793–1863)

ran away as a young man to live with
the Cherokee Indians. "The Raven," as
he was called by his adopted brothers,
returned with heavy heart to the frontier
village of Maryville, Tennessee, to pay
his debts. He taught school and fought
bravely under Andrew Jackson in the
War of 1812, but he never forgot the
Indians he had come to love. In 1818
Sam left the army and went on to study
law. He became a congressman and
then the governor of Tennessee. Later,
as the result of a strange series of
events, Sam moved on to the new
frontier of Texas. Here he became
commander-in-chief of the American
settlers who were fighting for independence from Mexico. As president of the
republic of Texas and later as governor,
Sam Houston became a symbol for
the newly admitted Lone Star State.

Sam Houston
Hero of Texas
by Jean Lee Latham

1. "Call Me 'Captain!'"

Sam waved his wooden sword and shouted "Halt!" He had six boys in his army. His little brother Willie was the youngest. His friend Tom was the oldest. But Sam was captain. He was bigger than Tom. Besides, he knew how to run an army. He was the son of a soldier. Father had fought in the Revolutionary War. He had helped America beat the British.

Lots of fathers and grandfathers had fought in the war. But they were not soldiers now. It was 1801, eighteen years since the war ended in 1783. Most men had left the army then. But father was still a soldier. He was Captain Sam Houston. He wasn't home very much. He rode from one fort to another. He had to see if the soldiers were doing things right.

Father had taught Sam to read out of *The Manual of Arms*. That was a book that told how to train soldiers. Sam could read "Halt!" and "Forward march!" and "Charge!" before he started to school.

Father called him "the best soldier of your size in Virginia."

Sam always saluted and said, "I'll be the next Captain Sam Houston!"

Every day Sam drilled his army around Timber Ridge. That was what father called his big plantation. Sam marched his army from the little stone church to the log schoolhouse. He marched them from the big white house to the woods. He always drilled them until time for school.

"Mark time!" he yelled. "One, two!" The boys stamped their feet.

Tom stopped. "Hey, Sam!"

"Call me 'Captain!' "

"Yes, sir. Hey, Captain! We're going to be late for school!"

Sam looked up at the sun. "Forward! Forward, my brave men! To the schoolhouse! Charge!"

The boys ran. Sam could have beaten them. He waited for Willie.

Willie grabbed Sam's hand. "Captain, sir, are we going to be late again?"

"Don't worry. I'll take the blame."

"What will the teacher say *this* time?"

Sam could guess what the teacher would say. "Sam Houston! Why can't you be like your older brothers? Why don't you set an example for Willie?"

It was hard to be the middle child of nine. Paxton and Robert and James and John were older. Willie and Mary and Isabelle and Eliza Ann were younger. Every day somebody said, "Mind your older brothers. Set an example for Willie."

The boys had reached the schoolhouse. They waited for Sam. Just as Sam got there, the teacher opened the door. "Well, Sam?"

"It's my fault, sir."

The teacher sighed. "Sam Houston! Why can't you be like your older brothers? I don't know what will become of you."

"I know," Sam thought. "I'll be the next Captain Houston." But he did not say it. He said again, "It's my fault, sir." He led his army into the school.

Two years later father became Major Houston. Sam was proud enough to burst. Someday *he* would be the next Major Houston.

In 1807, when Sam was fourteen, father died suddenly. After the funeral mother called the children together. She said to them, "Father owed a lot of money. He sold Timber Ridge to pay his debts. All we have left is some land in Tennessee." She looked at her family. "We will go there and start a new life. I know you'll mind Robert and help all you can."

Sam thought, "Robert will be bossing me." Robert was nineteen. Paxton was older, but he was sick.

Robert looked at Sam. "Well, Sam? How about it?"

Sam took a deep breath. He saluted. "Yes, sir!"

2. The Raven

Sam said "yes, sir," to Robert all the way to Knoxville, Tennessee. He said "yes, sir," through the little town of Maryville. He said "yes, sir," till they reached father's land. It was ten miles from Maryville. Sam looked around him at all the trees. It would be fun to live in the woods.

"Now," Robert said, "we *really* get to work."

Sam threw back his shoulders again. "Yes, sir!"

He helped cut down trees to build their home. They built two log cabins with a roofed-over place between them. They plowed. They planted corn. Soon green shoots poked through the ground.

Robert and Sam worked together on their land to build log cabins like this one.

Robert gave Sam a hoe. "You'll take care of the corn, Sam. Keep the weeds chopped out."

Sam yelled, "No! I hate farming! Why do I have to do it?"

"James and John must help me clear more land. You've got to do something to be worth your salt."

"I won't be a farmer."

Robert thought a minute. He said, "Mr. Weber wants a clerk in his store in Maryville. Can we depend on you to do that?"

"Anything's better than farming."

But working in the store was worse. Sam hated to be shut in all day. He hated to sweep and weigh. Finally Sam ran off. He didn't take anything but some food, his favorite books, and his musket.

Four days later he was in a Cherokee Indian village on Hiwassee Island in the Hiwassee River. Most of these Cherokees could speak English. They lived in log houses and raised corn, beans, and squash. But Sam did not see any men hoeing corn.

Chief Oo-loo-te-ka said, "So you want to live here. What can you do?"

Sam slapped his gun. "I can fight."

Oo-loo-te-ka said, "We live at peace. My name means 'He-Puts-the-Drum-Away.'"

"I can hunt."

Oo-loo-te-ka shook his head. "A musket makes too

much noise. You would scare the game." He pointed
to a slim tree. "Hit it three times."

Sam shot and hit the tree. He started to reload his
musket.

"Quickly!" Oo-loo-te-ka said.

"Just as soon as I've loaded it again."

An Indian boy shot five arrows into the tree. They
were in a straight line, one under the other. Sam
wasn't ready to fire his second shot yet. The boy
handed Sam his bow and an arrow.

Sam pulled back on the bowstring. He stopped in
surprise. How stiff the bow was! He jerked back on
the string. The arrow slipped from his fingers. It
missed the tree by a yard.

The Indian men said nothing. A little boy of nine
or ten looked at Sam with dancing eyes.

Sam pointed to the boy's small bow. "Let's see you
shoot."

"My arrows cannot go as far." The little boy went
closer to the tree. He shot. His arrow hit the tree in
line with the others.

Sam grinned at him. "Little brother, *you* shall teach
me to shoot."

Suddenly all of the Indians were smiling.

Oo-loo-te-ka lifted his hand. "Hear me! This is my
son, Co-lon-neh." He said, "That means 'the Raven.'
It is a good-luck bird of my people."

Young Sam Houston (left) in the clothing of a Cherokee. He lived with the Cherokees (below) for three years as an adopted son.

Sam bowed. "The Raven shall try to be worthy of his name."

"Can The Raven run?" Oo-loo-te-ka asked.

Sam grinned. He pointed to a tree about 100 yards away. Four boys lined up to race. Sam beat them all.

The Indians cheered.

"How far can my son run in a day?" Oo-loo-te-ka asked.

"In a *day*? I never *tried* to run a whole day. How far can your men run?"

"Twenty-five miles. Our best runners can do better. They can run fifty miles in a day."

"Little Brother," Sam said, "you can teach me to run too."

The Indians laughed. Sam knew they were laughing with him and not at him. He laughed too. He felt at home.

3. I.O.U.

That fall the whole village went hunting. By then Sam could use a bow and arrow. He could run all day. He could move through the forest as quietly as an Indian.

One day in November a tall boy walked into the store in Maryville. He wore buckskin trousers and moccasins. He was almost as brown as an Indian. His hair was long. A headband kept it out of his eyes. His hair was brown, and his eyes were gray.

Mr. Weber stared. "Sam Houston!"

"My name is The Raven." Sam laid two deer skins on the counter. He gave Mr. Weber a slip of paper. "The Raven will buy these things with his deer skins."

Mr. Weber read the list. "Your deer skins will not pay for all these things. You'll still owe $35.00."

"I must have presents for my friends." Sam wrote on a piece of paper. "I.O.U. $35.00. Sam Houston." He said, "Next time The Raven shall bring more skins."

Mr. Weber rubbed his chin. "I guess it's all right. Your brothers are part owners of the store now. I guess they'll pay your debts if you don't."

"The Raven will pay his own debts!"

From time to time Sam came back to the store. He brought more skins. He bought more presents. He signed more I.O.U.'s.

Three years passed. Again Sam came to the store. Two Indian boys were with him. They were tall, but they did not come to Sam's chin. Sam was over six feet tall.

"The Raven has brought his brothers to help carry his presents," Sam said.

Mr. Weber and two men in the store whispered together for a few moments.

Mr. Weber said, "No, Sam. No more presents. Not till you pay what you owe: $100.00."

"What!"

Behind Sam a man laughed. "What you going to do, Mr. Indian?"

Sam did not answer. He walked out of the store with his friends. "Tell Oo-loo-te-ka that The Raven must stay here for a while. He must pay a debt. Then he will come back." He watched the boys walk away.

A man across the street called, "Hey, Mr. Indian! Hear you're in a little trouble!"

Sam did not answer. He started home. That night he sat at his mother's table. He tried to eat. The food stuck in his throat.

After supper Robert said, "Well, Sam? What are you going to do?"

4. "Well, Sam?"

For a long time Sam didn't answer. He was afraid to speak. He didn't know what might happen. He might yell at Robert. He might bawl like a baby.

Robert said again, "Well, Sam? What are you going to do?"

Sam said quietly, "I'll pay my debt."

"How?"

"I don't know yet. But I'll pay it."

Willie smiled. "He'll do it, all right. Sam can do anything he sets his mind to."

Willie was fifteen now. He was springing up like a weed. He was going to the Porter Academy in Maryville. Everybody said he was doing fine.

"Next week," Willie said, "we're going to have a party in Maryville. People will come from all over the county. We'll have speeches and music and a spelling bee. Wouldn't you like to come?"

Sam looked at his buckskin trousers and moccasins.

Mother said, "We'll make you a new suit."

A week later Sam had a new suit of homespun. The shoemaker in Maryville had made shoes for him. How stiff they felt!

He went to the party. As he walked in he heard a buzz of whispers.

"Hey, Mr. Indian," a man asked, "do you know white man's talk?"

Some people laughed.

"I'll bet I read more in a week than he reads in a year," Sam thought. He had read his favorite books over and over. He knew whole pages by heart. He smiled at the man. "If I hear any words I don't know, I'll ask you."

The last thing on the program was the spelling bee. Willie was one of the captains to choose up sides.

"I want my brother Sam."

A man said, "Too bad to waste your first choice. He won't last long."

When the spelling bee ended, Sam had won.

People clapped. Someone said, "You ought to be a teacher!"

Sam spoke before he thought. "That's what I'm going to do—open a school."

The buzz of whispers began again.

A man said, "I might send my kids to you, if you're cheap enough. *Real* teachers charge six dollars a year. What'll you charge?"

Sam had held his temper a long time. He shouted, "I'll charge eight dollars."

The day came when Sam opened his school. He stood in an empty log cabin and waited. What was going to happen? Would anybody come?

5. "He Won't Last the Night"

Soon the schoolhouse was crowded. More pupils came. Sam had to turn them away. "I can pay my debt," he thought. "Next year I'll be back at Hiwassee Island. Nothing can stop me!"

Sam paid his debt, but he didn't go back to Hiwassee Island. That summer the War of 1812 began. America was fighting Great Britain again. The next spring Sam joined the army.

Mother did not weep when she said good-bye. She gave Sam his father's musket. "Never disgrace it, Sam. Never turn your back to save your life."

"I promise!" And Private Sam Houston marched away. He was only a common soldier now. But someday he would make his mother proud of him! He was sure of it.

Before long an officer noticed Sam. After all, Sam did know *The Manual of Arms* by heart. Soon he was Sergeant Houston, drilling other men.

The spring of 1814 he was Ensign Houston. He was going into his first battle. He was fighting under General Andrew Jackson. Jackson's men said he was the best leader in the war. They called him "Old Hickory."

Old Hickory was fighting the Creek Indians. The Creeks were fighting for the British. They had attacked a fort and killed every man, woman, and child. Old Hickory had been after them for months.

Now 1,000 Creek warriors were holed up at Horseshoe Bend on the Tallapoosa River. On two sides and behind, the deep river protected them. Across the open end of Horseshoe Bend the Creeks had built a thick breastwork of logs. For two hours Old Hickory's cannons hammered at it. They could not break through.

Now the drums beat the signal, "Charge!"

Sam Houston fought under Old Hickory and was wounded in the Indian wars.

Sam was the first man over the wall. He slashed his sword right and left. More men followed him. The Indians began to fall back. They hid in gullies and behind trees and rocks. They went on shooting.

Suddenly Sam realized he had been wounded. An arrow was sticking in his left leg above the knee. He tried to pull it out. He could not. He knew the arrow was barbed, like a fishhook. He turned to a soldier.

"Pull it out."

The soldier tried. "I can't."

Sam lifted his sword. *"Pull it out!"*

The soldier shut his eyes and jerked. The arrow came out. Blood spurted. Men helped Sam over the wall. They tied up the wound to stop the bleeding. They carried him away from the fighting and laid him on the ground. They went back to the fight. Sam tried to follow them, but he was too dizzy.

Late in the afternoon he got up, gritted his teeth, and limped back to the battle. The Indians were making one last stand. They were in a gully, behind another breastwork of logs.

"I'll not ask the men to charge," Old Hickory said. "I'll ask for volunteers."

Sam ran toward the breastwork. Two bullets hit his right side, one in the shoulder and one in his arm.

The next thing he knew it was dark. Someone was working on his arm.

"Got the bullets out, Doc?" someone asked.

"One. No use going after the other. He won't last the night. He's lost too much blood."

6. "You're Starting Late"

"I won't die," Sam muttered. *"I won't!"*

In the morning he was still alive. He heard men talking. What could they do with him? He'd never last to Fort Williams, they said. But they couldn't leave him here. Some men put him on a stretcher and started off.

Two months later soldiers brought him to his

mother's house. Mother looked at him, puzzled. Then she gasped, "Sam! It's you!"

Weeks passed before he could sit up. More weeks passed before he could walk. "I've got to get well faster!" he said. "I've got to get back to the army. If I don't, they'll dismiss me."

A letter came for Sam. He had been promoted to lieutenant. There was a note from General Jackson, too. Old Hickory remembered him. For the first time Sam grinned.

Early in 1815 the fighting ended. The army began to dismiss men left and right. They dismissed Sam's whole regiment. But they did not dismiss Sam. They sent him to another regiment.

"Maybe," Sam thought, "Old Hickory still remembers me."

Later in 1817 a major sent for Sam. "Lieutenant Houston, I have special orders for you. General Jackson says you're the man for the job."

Old Hickory still remembered him!

"The United States has bought land from the Cherokees. But we're having trouble with some of the chiefs. They won't move west and give up the land. Of course, we could send a regiment in and *make* them go. But we don't want that. You're to talk to them. Get them to go peaceably. You'll leave at once for Hiwassee Island."

Sam wanted to shout, "No!" But he could not. He was a soldier. He had his orders. He went.

"My son!" Oo-loo-te-ka said. "You have come home." He paused. "But a cloud hangs over my son. What is it?"

Sam told him.

Sam carried out his orders. The Indians moved west to the Arkansas River country.

In June of 1818 Sam was in Nashville. He stood in the law office of Mr. James Trimble.

"You want to become a lawyer?" Mr. Trimble stared. "I thought you were in the army."

"I resigned, sir."

"Odd. I heard you were doing very well. How old are you?"

"Twenty-five, sir."

"You're starting late." Mr. Trimble looked up at the rows of heavy books. "Well, you may read law in my office. But it'll be a long time before you'll be ready to pass your examinations."

"How long, sir?"

"At least eighteen months. Maybe you'll be ready by the end of 1819. You'll be almost 27 then, and not even started. Just ready to start."

"Eighteen months. . . ."

"*If* you work hard," Mr. Trimble said, "very hard."

"Don't worry, sir. I'm going to work."

7. "A Man I Can Trust"

Sam passed his law examinations in six months. Before the end of 1819 he was attorney general of the Nashville District and Colonel Houston of the Tennessee Militia.

In 1823 Major General Houston was in Washington, a congressman from Tennessee. In 1827 he was governor of his state.

By 1828 people were talking of bigger things for Sam. Old Hickory had been elected president. "You'll be the next president, Sam," men said. "Nothing can stop you!"

But early in 1829 a tall, bearded man rode into Oo-loo-te-ka's village on the Arkansas River.

"My son!" the old chief said.

"The Raven has come home."

Oo-loo-te-ka did not ask questions. But that night Sam told him. "I have not told this to any white man. I never shall. But I shall tell you. Not long ago I was married. Then I found out my wife loved someone else. Her family had made her marry me, because they thought I might be the next president of the United States."

"The Raven is welcome as long as he wants to stay."

Sam said, "The Raven will never again walk among white men."

But three years later Sam went to Washington. He went for the sake of the Cherokees. He told Old Hickory how some of the government agents had been cheating the Cherokees.

Old Hickory checked on the agents. He fired several. Then he asked, "Now what are you going to do, Sam?"

"I'll go back to the Cherokees. They need me."

"I need you too, Sam. I need a man I can trust. I want you to go to Texas for me."

He told Sam what had happened in Texas. Texas belonged to Mexico. But only a few Mexicans lived in Texas. Most of the white settlers were Americans.

"It's been a good bargain for the Mexicans," Old Hickory said. "The settlers have fought the Indians for them. A great many of our people have gone to Texas and become Mexican citizens. It looked like a bargain to them. They got good land for very little money. Now Mexico has passed a law that forbids any more Americans to settle in Texas. And the rulers of Mexico are doing everything they can to annoy the Americans who are already there."

"Why do the Texans put up with them?" Sam asked.

"There are fewer than 30,000 Texans, and there are about 8,000,000 Mexicans," Old Hickory said. "Texas has no army. If war began, I know what would happen. Many volunteers would come a-running. They'd fight a battle or two. Then they would go home. You can't win a war that way. I went through that sort of trouble in the War of 1812. Only trained soldiers will stick. Only trained men will obey."

"What do you think I can do in Texas?" Sam asked.

"Be my eyes and ears. Find out how the Texans feel. Find out what's going to happen."

8. Santa Anna

Sam rode slowly toward a town called Nacogdoches in eastern Texas. "First, I must get to know the people," he thought. "That will take time. Then. . . ."

"Sam Houston!" a man called. It was a man from Tennessee.

In half an hour Sam was talking with three dozen men. "We need you," they said.

Sam felt a warm glow. "Why?"

Then an argument started. Texas seemed to be split into a "Peace Party" and a "War Party."

The men from the Peace Party said, "Sam, you have been a congressman and a governor. You can help us get along with Mexico."

The men from the War Party said, "Bah! You can help us fight against the Mexicans!"

"Do you have an army?" Sam asked.

They laughed. "Don't you worry. Any Texan can lick 50 Mexicans."

Sam promised to come back. He rode west. He stopped in towns along the way. He went as far as San Antonio. When he got back to Nacogdoches he had ridden over 1,000 miles.

But how little he'd seen of Texas! A man could ride for a year and never see half of it. He stopped just outside Nacogdoches. He drew a deep breath. Texas was the place for him. He'd never feel shut in. Here a man could start a new life. Sam decided to stay.

He became a Texan and opened a law office. He wrote to Old Hickory how he felt about Texas. He ended his letter, "I believe nine-tenths of the Texans want to rebel against Mexico. If they won their independence they would want to join the United States."

"*If* they won their independence," he thought. How could they ever do that?

In the fall of 1835, war began. General Santa Anna was the president of Mexico then. He sent a regiment into Texas with orders: All Texans were to give up their guns. Any man found bearing arms would be shot.

Even the Peace Party shook fists and yelled. Texans depended on hunting for much of their food. How could they hunt without guns? How could they protect themselves against Indian raids?

Texans called a convention to form a government. Every town sent a man. Nacogdoches sent Sam. The

Santa Anna, president of Mexico, tried to put down the uprising of settlers from the United States.

convention elected him commander-in-chief of their army.

"What army?" Sam thought.

Volunteers did not wait for an army to be organized. They "came a-running." They fought the Mexicans and drove them out. They thought that the war was over.

"The war has not even begun!" Sam told them. "Santa Anna will come. He will wait till spring when the grass is up. He will need food for his horses and mules. But he'll come by March 1. We must be ready for him!"

The volunteers said "Bah!" Over 200 men went south with Dr. Grant and Colonel Johnson. They were going to capture Matamoros in Mexico. Other volunteers went home.

Sam argued. He pleaded. He swore. The government got tired of him. It made Colonel Fannin the commander-in-chief.

The government ordered Sam north. He was to talk to the Indians in northeastern Texas. He was to get their promise that they would not help the Mexicans.

9. The Alamo

Sam rode north. His friend Major Hockley rode with him.

At last Hockley spoke. "Can you get back in time for the next convention? It meets March 1 at Washington-on-the-Brazos."

"I bet the members of the convention are hoping I can't."

They found the Indians. Sam got their promise not to help the Mexicans. He and Hockley started back at a gallop. Hockley's horse went lame.

Sam didn't stop. "I'll see you in Washington-on-the-Brazos!" he yelled.

On March 1 Sam strode into the convention.

Men jumped up, and they crowded around him. Were they going to throw him out?

"General Houston! Thank heaven you're here!" Sam had been right, they said. Santa Anna had come. He was attacking the Alamo. Colonel Travis and 150 Texans were trapped there.

"Oh, no!" Sam had seen the Alamo. It was a mission near San Antonio. Sometimes the Alamo was used as a fort. Travis could never hold it with 150 men. "What have you done?"

"He sent a call for help. We hope our men have answered it."

"What men?" Sam asked. "Where are Grant and Johnson? On their way to Mexico?"

"They gave that up. Too many men deserted. Last we heard, they were hunting wild horses."

"Where's your commander-in-chief?"

Men looked at their boots. "Fannin's at Goliad. We're *sure* he's gone to help Travis. And Fannin has 400 men, all trained soldiers, from the United States."

"I know," Sam said. "They're men I sent for."

Again the men studied their boots.

The next day the Texans declared their independence from Mexico. They set to work to organize a government. They re-elected Sam commander-in-chief. Another message came from the Alamo. Only 32 men had answered the call for help. They were from

Gonzales, a town 70 miles from the Alamo. Fannin had sent no men. So Travis had fewer than 200 soldiers. He was running out of ammunition.

Sam sent orders to Grant and Johnson and Fannin: "Join me at Gonzales." He galloped out of town. Hockley and three others rode along.

At dawn the next morning, Sam put his ear to the ground. He listened. "We're too late. If they were still fighting, I could hear the guns. The Alamo has fallen. *Come on!*"

Near Gonzales the road was crowded with Texans carrying guns.

Travis and his men fought bravely at the Alamo, but they could not withstand the Mexican attack.

"We heard there was shooting again," one man said. "So we came a-running. Where's the fight?"

Sam said, "Major Hockley, get these men organized. Start drilling them!" He dashed on alone into the town.

People crowded around him. Was there any news from the Alamo?

"No word yet," Sam told them.

Four days later they knew. Santa Anna had killed every man at the Alamo. Now he would march on Gonzales. He had 7,000 men.

A scout brought word of Grant and Johnson. A Mexican army had attacked them. A few of their soldiers had escaped. The rest of the men were dead.

Sam could wait no longer for Fannin. He must leave Gonzales right away. He sent Fannin orders where to meet him. That night Gonzales was empty. The army moved slowly. They had to take care of the townspeople.

A scout brought more bad news. Fannin would not come. He was going to hold Goliad.

"Hockley," Sam said, "we'll never see poor Fannin again. Get ready to march."

He looked at his rag-taggle army. It was the last hope of Texas. He could not risk a battle yet. He must retreat. How the Texans were going to hate that!

10. San Jacinto

Sam marched his men in a crazy zigzag, north, then east, then south, then north again. He had to dodge the armies he could not beat. "We came to *fight!*" the men said. Some deserted.

One night a ragged soldier crawled into Sam's camp. He had been one of Fannin's men. Fannin had finally started out from Goliad, but it had been too late. A Mexican army had surrounded him.

"We surrendered," the soldier whispered. "They marched us back to Goliad. Then Santa Anna sent orders to shoot us. They marched us out of the town and shot us down like dogs. I got away. I don't know if any others did."

That night 100 men deserted.

Now and then more volunteers joined. Once Sam had 600 men. What chance would they have against 7,000?

One thing gave Sam hope. Santa Anna's armies were not together. They were spread out on a front 100 miles wide.

Still Sam retreated and did not fight. More men deserted. Other volunteers joined him. At last, on April 21, 1836, he faced Santa Anna by the San Jacinto River. Sam had fewer than 800 men. Santa Anna had more than 1,300. The Mexicans had made a barricade of baggage and wagons in front of their camp.

The Texans knew the time had come to fight. Why didn't General Houston give the order to attack? All day they grumbled and waited. It was after three o'clock when Sam called them together. He gave them their orders. He gave them a battle cry, too: "Remember the Alamo! Remember Goliad!"

The Texans started silently across the plain toward Santa Anna's camp. Sam rode back and forth in front of them. "Hold your fire! Hold your fire!"

The Mexicans fired. Sam's horse fell. He yelled again. "Hold your fire!" He mounted another horse. He raced back and forth, yelling, "Hold your fire!" That horse fell too. "Hold your fire!" Sam mounted a third horse. At last he yelled, "Remember the Alamo! Fire!"

The Texans had caught the Mexicans off guard. They were lounging around camp. Some were playing cards. Some were asleep. The battle did not last half an hour. The Mexicans surrendered.

Sam rode back to camp. Suddenly he was dizzy. Hockley grabbed him as he fell from his saddle.

The next thing Sam knew a doctor was working on his leg. "Both bones are smashed," the doctor said, "just above the ankle."

"Did we get Santa Anna?" Sam asked.

No, his men said, there was no sign of him.

"Keep hunting! Look for someone dressed as a common soldier. He'll probably be crawling away on all fours."

The next day Sam's men brought in one more Mexican. He looked like a common soldier. But the other prisoners gasped, "El presidente!"

A roar went up from the Texans. They knew "el presidente" meant "the president." They had captured Santa Anna! Texas was free! The war was over!

The doctor was frowning at Sam's leg. "We've got to get you to New Orleans. We can't take care of you here."

"I can't leave," Sam said. "I have things to do."

It was a month later when Sam got to New Orleans. The doctor there swore when he saw the leg.

Three weeks later the doctor was storming at Sam again. "You *can't* go back to Texas yet. Do you want to kill yourself?"

"I have things to do."

Sam got as far as a little town near Nacogdoches. Once again someone grabbed him as he fell from his saddle. Soon another doctor was growling at him.

"You're going to stay in bed for at least a month. You'll stay if I have to tie you down."

The Texans elected Sam president. He got over 4,000 votes. The next highest man got less than 800.

General Sam Houston, wounded in battle, accepts the surrender of the defeated *presidente*.

"You're in no condition to take on that job," the doctor said. "Wild men have been swarming into Texas. It'll take a man of iron to run this country. It'll be worse than fighting a war."

"I won't have to rule Texas very long," Sam told him. "The United States will take us into the Union."

But the United States said "No!" The North was fighting tooth and nail against admitting Texas. Another slave state? Never!

11. Two Monuments

Nine years later, in 1845, the United States admitted Texas. Sam felt as though he had just laid down a heavy load. He had been president of Texas twice. The doctor had been right. It had taken a man of iron to rule Texas.

Now he could have time to enjoy his family. He was married to a beautiful young woman from Alabama. He and Margaret had a little son.

"Now I'll have time to rest and enjoy little Sam," he said.

Margaret smiled. "You'll enjoy little Sam. I don't think you'll rest."

Sam was elected senator from Texas. "I'll be lonely in Washington," he said.

"But you'll go," Margaret said. "Texas needs you."

The admission of Texas into the United States led to war with Mexico. When the war ended, America owned Texas, California, and all the land between them.

Sam knew there was danger of another war. The trouble between the North and the South was getting worse. He was a southerner, but he believed in the Union. For years, as senator, Sam fought to hold the Union together.

In 1859 Texas elected him governor. Day after day Sam made speeches in favor of the Union. Some people cheered. Others booed.

In February of 1861, Texas left the Union and joined the South. Sam walked the floor. "What can I do, Margaret? Will I turn against my country or turn against my state?"

"You'll do what you think is right," she said.

"If I don't promise to be true to the South, Texas will throw me out of the governor's chair."

"I've never seen you back down yet," Margaret said.

Sam let his beloved Texas throw him out of office. He went home to the little town of Huntsville.

"You'll have time for us now," the children said.

Sam grinned and hugged each one of them. He had eight children now. There were Sam, Jr., four little girls, then three more little boys. Andy was seven, Willie was three, and Temple was a baby.

Sam Houston—great warrior and statesman—as he was photographed during his later years.

"Willie and I have fun," Andy said.

"I know," Sam said. "I had a brother named Willie."

In April the war began. "All at once," Sam thought, "I feel 100 years old."

The summer of 1863 he fell ill. "It's nothing," he said. "I'll get over it. I've got to! When the war's over, Texas will need me." But in July he died.

Today a tall monument in San Jacinto marks the place where Sam saved Texas. But the oldest monument to Sam Houston is a little log cabin near Maryville, Tennessee. It is the log schoolhouse where Sam "paid his own debt."

Index

and farming, 134
and first marriage, 147
and Andrew Jackson, 142, 145, 147, 148–149
and military career, 129 (pic), 142, 146, 147, 150–158
and move to Tennessee, 132–133
and move to Texas, 149
political career of, 147, 158, 160–161
as schoolteacher, 141
and Texas Revolution, 150–158, 159 (pic), 160
and War of 1812, 142, 143, 144, 145
Houston, Sam (father of Sam Houston), 130, 132
Houston, Sam (son of Sam Houston), 161
Houston, Temple (son of Sam Houston), 161, 163
Houston, Willie (brother of Sam Houston), 130, 131, 140
Houston, Willie (son of Sam Houston), 161, 163
Hunters and hunting, 15, 16, 20, 35, 102–103, 107–108, 112, 135

I

Indians
Cherokees, 23, 25, 134, 135, 136 (pic), 137, 139, 145, 148
Chickasaws, 112
Creeks, 104, 105, 116, 142
and French and Indian War, 16
and hunting grounds, 16–17, 23
and land treaties, 23, 25, 30, 116
raids by, 20, 21, 22, 23, 27 (pic), 33, 34, 64, 65 (pic), 72, 104
and Revolutionary War, 30, 34
Seminoles, 72, 73, 74
Shawnees, 26, 27, 30, 31
village life of, 11–12, 135, 137

J

Jackson, Andrew
appearance of, 49, 80 (pic)

and Battle of Horseshoe Bend, 64, 66
and Battle of New Orleans, 67, 69, 70–71 (pic), 72
becomes a judge, 59
becomes major general, 67
birth of, 48
and cattle drive, 50
childhood of, 46–48, 49, 50
death of, 81
and father, 47
as governor of Florida, 74
and horse racing, 60, 61
and House of Representatives, 59
as a lawyer, 56, 58, 59
and mother, 47, 49, 51, 55, 56
and move to Nashville, 57
nicknamed Old Hickory, 63
as president of the United States, 75 (pic), 77, 78, 79, 116
as prisoner of war, 54, 55 (pic)
and Revolutionary War, 50, 51, 52 (pic), 53
runs for presidency (1824), 74
and Seminole Indian War, 72, 73, 74
as senator from Tennessee, 74
and Tennessee Militia, 45 (pic), 59, 62, 63, 64, 66
Jackson, Andrew, Jr. (son of Andrew Jackson), 62
Jackson, Bobby (brother of Andrew Jackson), 47, 50, 51, 53, 54, 55
Jackson, Hugh (brother of Andrew Jackson), 47, 50
Jackson, Rachel Donelson (wife of Andrew Jackson), 58, 59, 60 (pic), 61, 74, 76
Jefferson, Thomas, 78
Johnson, Francis W., 152, 153, 154, 155

K

Kentucky
explored by Daniel Boone, 18, 19 (pic), 21
settlement of, 26, 34
sold by Indians, 25, 26

DATE DUE

920

WAYNE, BENNETT

AUTHOR

MEN OF THE WILD FRONTIER

TITLE

DATE DUE	BORROWER'S NAME
APR 2	Donnie
	Mr Overly
OCT 23 '79	Rosemary Jeffrey
DEC 20 '79	Dave Cunningham

920

WAYNE, BENNETT

"MEN OF THE WILD FRONTIER"